# Brunel

# Brunel

Annabel Gillings

HAUS PUBLISHING • LONDON

Originally published in Great Britain in 2006 by
Haus Publishing Limited
26 Cadogan Court
London SW3 3BX

**www. hauspublishing.co.uk**

Copyright © Annabel Gillings 2006

The moral right of the author has been asserted

A CIP catalogue record for this book
is available from the British Library

ISBN 1-904950-44-2 (paperback)

Designed and typeset in Garamond by Falcon Oast Graphic Art Ltd.
Printed and bound by Graphicom in Vicenza, Italy

Front cover: Topham Picturepoint
Back cover: Topham Picturepoint

# Contents

# Birth and Revolution

On 9 April 1806, Isambard Kingdom Brunel was born. The name Kingdom was that of his mother's English family, while Isambard and Brunel were products of his father's French lineage. Despite his grand name, he arrived into a quite ordinary terraced house in Portsea, a suburb of Portsmouth.

Isambard was the third child of Sophia and Marc Brunel, but the first boy and consequently, in the 19th century, the first who could follow Marc into his beloved profession: engineering.

Years later, Isambard Kingdom Brunel's unusual name would become almost synonymous with engineering: he was perhaps the most eminent Victorian engineer. He built more than 1,000 miles of railway across Britain; he designed over 100 daring and elegant bridges on a vast scale; he created the first prefabricated field hospital for soldiers of the Crimean War (yet he also advanced the design of guns); he revolutionised ship design and he built the most enormous and advanced vessels the world had ever seen. Thousands emigrated to Australia and America on ships built by Brunel. His work altered the lives of almost every person in Britain, and millions abroad. It is still integral to our transport system and can be seen in Paddington Station; the Clifton Suspension Bridge in Bristol; the Royal Albert Bridge at Saltash and by anyone who uses a train in the west of Britain today.

Brunel's achievements were enormous; a product of his prodigious energy and vision. Yet this incredible ambition would come to threaten not only Brunel's work, but also ultimately to endanger his own life.

That ambition began with Brunel's father, Marc; in spite of his gentle manner he would exert the greatest influence on Brunel's life. The events and work of Marc's life were a powerful force in shaping those of Isambard.

Marc Brunel was a famous engineer in his own right, but it was a position for which he had to work hard. He was born in the small village of Hacqueville, Normandy, in 1769. As the youngest son, his father expected him to train for the priesthood. But Marc hated Latin and Greek, and much preferred drawing, maths and carpentry. His creativity was obvious, but his father could see no future in it. So despite his protestations, Marc was sent to train at the Seminary of St Nicaise in Rouen.

Fortunately for Marc, the Principal of St Nicaise recognised his talents and persuaded Marc's father of them. When he was 13, Marc was removed from the seminary and went to live with the Carpentier family, friends of the Brunels. Francois Carpentier was the American Consul at Rouen and a retired sea captain, who drew upon his naval connections, getting tutelage for Marc from his friend Professor Dulague, with the aim of Marc joining the navy as an officer cadet. For Marc, this opened up fantastic opportunities, since Dulague was also Professor of Hydrography at the Royal College of Rouen. Impressed by Marc, in 1786 he used his contacts with the Minister of Marine to secure for Marc the position of junior officer to a new frigate.[1] And so Marc began a six-year tour of duty, sailing to the West Indies, and America.

During this time Marc not only learned to speak English but gained invaluable experience in technical drawing and mathematics – he became fluent in the theories fundamental to engineering. These latter theories were not yet taught in England, and in due course, they were something that Marc would impress upon Isambard. But in 1789, during Marc's spell with the French navy, his travels were dramatically interrupted by the uprisings of the French Revolution. Marc was forced to return to Paris when

Sir Marc Isambard Brunel, father of the more famous Isambard Kingdom Brunel

French involvement in the Seven Years War and American Revolution combined with poor crops after 1787's bleak winter rendered France almost bankrupt. Still, Louis XVI and Marie Antoinette lived extravagantly and taxed the common man to the hilt, taking 70 per cent of his earnings. Peasant uprisings all over France culminated in Parisian workers storming the Bastille – Paris' prison and symbol of the monarchy's power – on 14 July 1789. By August, the National Assembly of Estates General consisting of clergy, nobles and the bourgeoisie, had drawn up a 'Rights of Man' declaration demanding liberty and equality. But the King refused to acknowledge it.

his frigate was sold off in 1792. A staunch royalist, he made an ill-advisedly public speech criticising Robespierre, and the angry crowd tried to seize him. He was forced to return to Rouen, where he took refuge with the Carpentier family.

Here, in the dark context of the Revolution, Marc met with a wonderful coincidence. Also staying with the Carpentiers at that time was Sophia Kingdom, the youngest of 16 children, now orphaned. Her father, William Kingdom, had been a naval contractor but died when Sophia was young, at which point her eldest brother became her guardian. With impeccably bad timing this brother sent Sophia to Rouen to learn French with the Carpentiers just as the French Revolution was getting started.

Sophia and Marc met in these tense circumstances, and quickly fell in love. After just a few months, Marc proposed and Sophia accepted. But once again, the Revolution intervened in Marc's life. Rouen – once a royalist enclave – was taken by the Jacobins and Marc and Sophia were forced to live in hiding.

The violence in the streets was intensifying, following the beheading of King Louis XVI. When Marc sarcastically addressed his dog as 'Citoyen' (citizen) in the street[2] in front of a patriot, the danger of his position became clear to him. He had to leave France or face imprisonment or even death.

Francois Carpentier was able to get a passport for Marc from the American Consulate allowing Marc to escape to New York on board the American ship *Liberty*, on 7 July 1793. But even on board, Marc was not yet safe. In August, after weeks at sea, a French frigate approached and searched the *Liberty* for runaways. As they approached, Marc found that he had lost his all-important passport. It took two hours for the French soldiers to find him, but in that time he had forged a new one. His skills in draughtsmanship paid off, and the soldiers fell for the forgery. He had escaped, but he had also left his precious Sophia behind in France.

Marc landed in New York on 6 September. He found work as an architect and engineer, and over the six years he stayed in America his reputation grew. He submitted the winning design for a new Congress Building at Washington (although it was not built in the end); he surveyed lakes and canals; and he became Chief Engineer of New York, designing a cannon foundry and advising on the defences of Long Island and Staten Island. He even took American citizenship. His dreams of returning to the French navy were forgotten in favour of his new career as an engineer.

But in France, things weren't going so well for Sophia. A decree was made in October 1793 that all English residents should be arrested and imprisoned. Besides her conspicuous

In 1791, the civil unrest in France had escalated; Louis XVI fled, but was captured and returned to Paris. A new constitution was duly declared; by September 1792 the royal family were imprisoned and the French Republic was declared. On 21 January 1793 the King was executed for treason to his people. So ensued the Reign of Terror where the Jacobins established a dictatorship, led by Maximilien Robespierre. Some 40,000 people were eventually beheaded. A government of five directors – The Directory – was established to rule France, overthrown by army general Napoleon Bonaparte in a coup d'etat in 1799. In 1804 Napoleon crowned himself Emperor of France.

Englishness, it was known that Sophia was engaged to an escaped royalist. She was taken away and locked up in a commandeered convent, where she and other prisoners slept on cramped beds of wooden boards, and were fed on bread mixed with straw.[3]

Sophia's imprisonment lasted until Robespierre fell in August 1794. At last she was able to return to England.

Marc and Sophia kept up a correspondence, and in 1798, chance offered them another opportunity to meet. It began when Marc was dining with Alexander Hamilton, a former aide to George Washington. A Frenchman, M. Delagibarre, who had just arrived from England, was another guest at the dinner. While discussing the Royal Navy's role in opposing the revolution, Deligabarre outlined their problematic shortage of pulleys, 1,400 of which were needed for one 74-gun ship.[4] At present, Delagibarre explained, the English method of making pulleys was a slow and expensive one, with most of the work done by hand. Marc saw a great business opportunity in improving the process. So, on 20 January 1799 Marc left New York for England with the intent of overhauling the pulley-making business.

Marc reached Falmouth in March and wasted no time in finding Sophia. He went straight to London, where she was living with her brother. After six years of separation, on 16 March they were finally together again, physically changed but still determined to be together. On 1 November of the same year they were married at the church of St Andrews in Holborn. In 1800 they had their first child, Sophia, and in 1805 another girl, Emma, before Isambard was born in 1806.

Marc and Sophia had a wonderfully happy marriage, but for them and their children, it was not always a stable household. Money was always a problem. Although Marc was astonishingly inventive – perhaps more so than his son would be – his business ventures were not always successful because he paid far more attention to ideas than to profits or accounting. In due course, this would have a great impact on Isambard; the desire for financial success would become one of the driving forces in his ambition.

Marc's first enterprise in England, the pulley-making business, got underway when he met Henry Maudsley, a man who would become the 'greatest mechanic of his age'.[5] At that point, Henry had a tiny shop in Wells St, off Oxford Street in London. But in time, it would spawn the screw-cutting lathe, the planing machine and the micrometer, and grow into perhaps the most famous engineering firm of the 19th century – one with which Isambard Kingdom Brunel would also come to do a great deal of work.

Marc's idea was to automate the process of making pulleys as much as possible, and he got Maudsley to make models of his designs for pulley-making machines. Next, Marc had to get the Navy to commission the full-scale version. Things didn't look hopeful: Sir Samuel Bentham, Inspector-General of the Naval Works, was already planning a pulley-making plant for Portsmouth Dockyard. But on seeing Marc's designs he recognised their brilliance, and dropped his own.

Marc's designs represented probably the first example of fully mechanized production in the world; the work previously done by 60 men could now be done by just six. A total of 43 different parts worked together to turn out the pulleys. The machines became famous and once complete, people came to marvel at them even from outside the Navy. Among them was Tsar Alexander I, who was so impressed that he asked Marc to come and work for him in St Petersburg, offering him a diamond ring as an inducement.[6] This offer would later prove very significant in the Brunels' fortunes.

Back in Portsmouth, Marc and Bentham agreed that Maudsley would build the machines and Marc would oversee their installation at Portsmouth. And so in 1802, Marc and Sophia moved to the small house in Portsea close to the dockyard, where their son Isambard was later born.

The pulley-making machines began a pattern that would repeat in Marc Brunel's life: that of a great idea and much hard work, for a small reward. A dispute arose over who actually invented the machinery – Marc who designed it; Bentham who had commissioned it; or Maudsley who built it. In the end, Marc got £17,000 from the Admiralty, a much smaller sum than he had hoped for.

Although the profits were tiny, Marc's pulley-making machinery had nevertheless helped to make his reputation in England. And now he was ready for a new challenge. He came across a sawmill at Battersea and – just as with the pulleys – he saw the potential for streamlining a large operation by applying engineering and logic to the problem. Marc observed how huge amounts of timber were unloaded from ships at dockyards and then moved from place to place before sawing. He realised that he could improve the operation by mechanising it, and installing a sawmill on the spot. It should be a lucrative business – the war with Napoleon was underway, and the necessary shipbuilding required huge amounts of timber: over 2,000 trees for one 74-gun ship alone.

So, in 1808, when Isambard was two years old, the family moved to 4 Lindsey Row, Chelsea,[7] to be near the Battersea sawmill. This house, backing on to the Thames, provided the backdrop to Brunel's childhood. He learnt to row on the river and to swim in it (indeed swallowing mouthful after mouthful of its filthy water possibly weakened his body from an early age). These were extremely happy times for Brunel.

Brunel was raised by a father who was inventive, innovative and inspirational. What's more, Brunel grew up in the time when the Industrial Revolution was underway, instilling in him a sense of the formidable force of mechanisation, and the transforming power of engineering. Not only was Brunel born at the right time but in exactly the right place: Britain was at the forefront of industrialising change. To the young Brunel, anything must have seemed possible.

In 1809 Marc had yet another business idea: boots. The state of the British army's feet had caught his attention. Marc saw the soldiers returning to Portsmouth from the Napoleonic wars with cut and bloody feet. They had no proper boots; all they had to walk in were dirty rags. The soles of their army-issue boots had been packed with clay, which had dissolved in the wet conditions; the boots had then simply fallen apart.

Following the invention of machines capable of mass-production, factories were built and concentrated in towns. New machinery also meant there was less agricultural work, so populations in the towns swelled rapidly. The overall population in Britain doubled in Brunel's lifetime, from 10,686,000 in 1801 to 23,189,000 in 1861. Britain became the world's first predominantly urban society and – for a time – the 'workshop of the world'. The increased variety of cheaper goods created the consumer-oriented society, changing ideologies as well as commerce.

Marc decided that he could make better boots, by once again applying an automated process. By 1812 he had created machines to make 400 pairs a day – all operated by ex-soldiers, injured in the war.

The boot business was doing well – especially when Napoleon escaped from exile on Elba in 1814, and the fighting flared up again. But when Britain won the Battle of Waterloo in 1815, the war came to a sudden end, and so did the need for army boots. The government cut its order and Marc was left with the excess, since the government refused to take, or pay for the boots it had ordered. It took a year of Marc pestering the government for them to pay him just half the money they owed.

The boots incurred a great loss. Marc's financial situation was bleak. In August 1814, when Isambard was eight, it got worse. A fire broke out at the Battersea Sawmill and it was entirely destroyed. Marc was characteristically cheerful and optimistic at first – he decided he would rebuild the sawmill, only better. But when he visited his friend and city banker, Mr Sansom, the true gravity of the situation was revealed to him. Sansom was amazed at the 'most extraordinary jumble' which Marc had certainly 'not understood'.[8]

It turned out that Marc's business partner had been less than honest; Marc had never noticed. His lack of involvement in money matters meant that the Brunel family constantly swung between extremes in their fortunes. Isambard Kingdom Brunel grew up under a wavering threat of impoverishment, so that from the beginning he learnt the value of financial security, and above all, success.

Then, in 1821, when Brunel was 15 and financial matters didn't look as if they could get any worse, they did. After the losses from the boots and from the fire at the sawmill, Marc could no longer pay his creditors. On 14 May, he was taken to King's Bench Prison, Southwark and incarcerated for debt.

# Education and Apprenticeship

Despite their financial turmoil, Marc had always ensured that his son had the best education possible. He recognised Isambard's talents and nurtured them from an early age. Marc taught Isambard to draw when he was four, then geometry and mathematics, so that the young Brunel mastered Euclid when he was 11.[9] Marc fostered in Isambard his own habit of sketching any building of particular interest that he might come across (Marc called this the 'Engineer's Alphabet'); and also encouraged the ability to look at a building, assess its structure and faults and then calculate an on-the-spot estimate of how much longer it would last before collapsing. Isambard was given every opportunity that Marc had longed for, as an aspiring engineer.

The young Brunel was sent to Dr Morell's boarding school in Hove, where he studied classics. He amazed the other boys with his ability to predict, correctly, the imminent demise of buildings, and displayed his precocious abilities by making a survey of the town in his spare time.[10]

But at the age of 14, Isambard was taken away from Dr Morell's school. Marc held French schooling in high regard; since by 1820 the disturbances of the French Revolution were calmed and monarchy was restored, there was peace enough for Marc to send his English son to France. Isambard went first to the College of Caen in Normandy, to finish his formal education, and after that to the Lycee Henri-Quatre in Paris, which was famous for its teaching of mathematics.

Here in Paris, Isambard was distanced – and probably even

sheltered – from his father's imprisonment back in England. Always loyal, Sophia had insisted on going with Marc, and served his sentence with him. Together, they tried to make use of the time; Marc made drawings of new inventions, while Sophia would busy herself with chores such as darning Marc's stockings.[11]

Marc felt cruelly let down by the British government, who had failed to pay for their order of army boots, and then imprisoned him for being penniless. Although Marc appealed, he couldn't get the Chancellor to pay him. Marc wrote to his friend Dr Woollaston: "If I had been guilty of any crime against the State I could not be treated with more severity, not to say cruelty than I am . . . Nothing but the fortitude of my dearest Mrs B. that supports me at all."[12]

Finally, he decided to take advantage of the offer that Tsar Alexander of Russia had made him, on seeing his block-making machinery. He wrote to him, asking to 'work under the protections of a sovereign whose enlightenment and liberality seems to shine forth doubly in contrast with the callousness of the government at home'.[13] And, in England, he let it be known that this was what he had done.

The Duke of Wellington relayed to the British government the threat of losing Marc's talents to another country. At last, they took notice. The Chancellor of the Exchequer paid Marc £5,000 to clear his debts – on condition that he would stay in Britain, and not go to Russia. Marc accepted. But although the money cleared his debts, there was none left over and he was still penniless when he and Sophia were released in August 1821.

In this situation, Marc cannot have been able to afford his son's tuition. But Isambard seems to have been protected, and since his education wasn't interrupted there must have been someone, some benefactor, paying his school fees, it is still not known who.[14] Marc had the highest ambitions for his son, and arranged for him to sit the entrance exam to the highly prestigious Ecole

Polytechnique, a university specialising in science and mathematics, where the very best French civil and military engineers were trained. But Isambard's 's entry was blocked by his nationality – no Englishman could get in to this prized French institution.[15]

The Ecole Polytechnique, the renowned Parisian engineering school which Brunel's English birth barred him from

There was no option left for Isambard. In Britain, the only degrees available were in law, medicine or book-learning, as a preparation for entering the Church. The new professions being created by the Industrial Revolution, such as architecture or engineering, had neither academic training nor professional qualification.

So instead of a degree, Isambard embarked on an apprenticeship which was to have a life-long influence on him. He was sent to a mentor in Paris; a maker of watches and scientific instruments called Louis Breguet.[16] Here, he would learn within the most precise engineering practice of the time, clockmaking. Breguet was considered to be the best in his field. From him, Isambard learnt the value and the techniques of expert craftsmanship, and an indefatigable eye for detail; he would carry Breguet's emphasis on meticulous high standards with him throughout his career.

Isambard's stay in Paris came to an end in 1822. After his release from prison, Marc had opened a new office in the City, at 29 Poultry. It was tiny, and he employed only one clerk. He was quickly engaged on several projects, including two suspension bridges on the Ile de Bourbon (the Mascarenes) in the Indian Ocean, and needed his son back to help him in his office. So, at the age of 16, Isambard returned to England.

As an assistant to his father, Isambard continued his education in engineering. It was a great advantage that Marc was a renowned engineer – Isambard got to work on inspiring and high-profile projects. And while students would usually have to pay a large fee to an engineer for four to five years, to gain the experience necessary to join the Institute of Civil Engineers, Isambard didn't have to pay a penny.

The work was varied. Brunel helped his father on a range of projects besides the bridges on the Ile de Bourbon: a design for a canal at Panama; a rotary printing press; a floating pier for Liverpool Docks; a project with Augustus Charles Pugin to design a cemetery at Kensal Green, known as the 'Necropolis of London';

and an improvement of steam engines, to allow them to be used in marine applications.[17]

At this time, 1823, Marc began work on a new invention to rival steam power: the Gaz Engine (sic). He got the idea in the spring of 1823, at a meeting of the Royal Society, where he was a fellow. That fateful day, Marc heard Sir Humphrey Davy read a paper describing Michael Faraday's work on the liquefaction of gases. Faraday had managed to liquefy various gases – including carbon dioxide – by the application of pressure. According to Davy, reversing the process with just a small amount of heat (so turning the liquid carbon dioxide back into a gas) would produce a great expansion of gas, that could be used to drive machinery in the same way as does steam in an engine – but without any unpleasant black smoke.

Marc decided that he would be the one to make this engine a reality. This fantastical plan would ultimately cost the Brunels thousands of pounds and thousands more hours. But the great potential drove them both on. They were unaware that at the same time, the scientist Sadi Carnot was establishing the laws of modern thermodynamics that explained why the Gaz Engine could never work. Carnot had demonstrated that an engine could only produce the amount of energy that was put into it – it could transform energy, but it could not create it. But this would not become known to British engineers for decades.

And so the Brunels worked on, in enthusiastic ignorance. They took the idea seriously, and so did others – they got a grant from the Admiralty, and the Private Journal of Isambard Brunel reports that the great Faraday himself came to help:

*Tuesday 10th May 1825*

*. . . Mr Brand & Mr Faraday came down to Rotherhithe with me show'd them everything. Mr F remained to help me in an experiment – changed – failed – owing to not cooling properly. The vessel was very tolerably tight the lower glass leather leaked a little.*[18]

For Isambard, the years from 1822 to 1825 were relaxed and happy, working for his father, and socialising with his sister Sophia and her new husband, Benjamin Hawes. Isambard became good friends with his brother-in-law, despite their different callings. While Brunel remained almost entirely detached from politics throughout his career (with a couple of interesting exceptions) Benjamin intended to stand for Parliament for the Liberals. The two of them spent days together, rowing and walking as they talked.

But in this period of relative calm, Brunel grew impatient. His father had groomed him perfectly for a career as an engineer, and this, combined with his natural ambition, made him restless. He was impatient for fame and success; he worried about how he could make his mark.

Finally, his chance arrived, fittingly, through his father. In July 1824, Marc was appointed engineer of the Thames Tunnel, the first under-water crossing in the world, and the most ambitious engineering project of the time. This would be the final stage of Isambard's apprenticeship.

A new crossing was needed for the east end of the Thames to serve London's busy and rapidly expanding docks. In the 1820s, most passengers – approximately 3,700 a day – crossed the river to the docks on ferries, while wagons and carts had to make a two-mile detour to cross the river at London Bridge.[19]

Building a new bridge to accommodate the many high-masted ships would have been difficult, and would have brought traffic to a stop, so a tunnel was thought to be the best solution. Several attempts had been made to tunnel under the Thames, but the only previous attempt that made real progress was in 1802 when a tunnel between Rotherhithe and Limehouse was proposed by Robert Vazie, a Cornish engineer. Work was going well until they hit quicksand. The famous engineer Richard Trevithick was called in, but the tide broke through again and the project was abandoned.[20]

A contemporary engraving of the Thames Tunnel

No one could see a solution to the problem of tunnelling through such soft soil, which under a river was even greater, due to the downward pressure from the water above. How was it possible to stop the tunnel collapsing as you worked in it, and behind you once you had dug it?

The answer lay with a worm. Marc Brunel spotted *Teredo navalis* in the timber one day when he was working at Chatham Dockyard. He noticed that this worm, the bane of the shipbuilder's life, had a peculiarly effective method of burrowing through even the hardest timber. Its outer shell acted as sawing tools, cutting off wood for the worm to eat, but also as a protective housing. The worm ate the wood, converting it into faeces, which was expelled from its back end. But rather than this product going to waste, it formed a structural tunnel lining behind the worm, preventing it from collapsing and trapping the worm.

Marc saw the genius in the worm's design, and copied it as closely as he could, scaling it up in metal to a grand scale. On 20 January 1818, Marc Brunel patented this as his Great Shield. It was probably his most important and successful design.

The Great Shield consisted of 12 massive cast-iron frames, 21 feet and 4 inches high by 3 feet wide. Each of these frames was divided into three working cells, placed on top of each other. Each man operated a single unit of the shield, mining the rock and earth directly ahead of him. The shield protected him from above, below and the sides. Behind the shield, bricklayers sealed the tunnel with bricks as the equivalent of the worm faeces. Only the front was exposed, and Marc had limited even this risk: only a small portion of earth could be mined at a time. The amount of soil exposed was minimised by a series of boards, of which only one was open at a time. The miner would pull back the board, mine the ground behind it, screw the board onto the new face, and then start on a new section.

When all the boards in the three cells of a single frame had been moved forward, the whole frame was jacked up and moved

Marc Brunel's tunnelling shield allowed twelve men to work simultaneously

along the tunnel. This cellular structure gave the shield inherent strength, and if there was any collapse of earth, it could be contained to one cell. Bricklayers would follow behind the frame, lining the newly-exposed earth with at least 2ft 6in of brickwork, to protect it from collapse. Marc published his plans, and on 18 February 1824 he met with the Institute of Civil Engineers. The day after, a public meeting was held and the Thames Tunnel Company was formed to build the tunnel.[21]

Starting south of the Thames, Marc planned the course of his tunnel to run from Rotherhithe (just three-quarters of a mile from Trevithick's abandoned driftway), under the Thames to Wapping, near the junction of Wapping Lane and Wapping High Street. Marc followed the advice of geologists who recommended that if he dug the tunnel shallow (that is, close to the river bed of the Thames – just 14 feet below it at one point) then he would be able to dig through a layer of strong blue clay, and avoid the quicksands that had defeated Trevithick.

Marc's plan was to cut two tunnels, as a dual carriageway, through the limited width of the band of clay. If he could get his shield to work and successfully drive the tunnels from Rotherhithe to Wapping, he would have made the first public tunnel under a waterway.

The opening ceremony for the works was held on 2 March 1825, led by William Smith MP, also the Chairman of the Thames Tunnel Company.

*Got up very early and went to Rotherhithe with my father. All hard at work up to the last minute as usual in such cases. A stage was erected in front of the Curb the crowd began to collect very early. My father laid the first brick I the second Armstrong and Smith followed.*[22]

Once work was underway, Marc shut his office at 29 Poultry and moved his family from Chelsea to No 30 Bridge Street, Blackfriars. This was an unfashionable neighbourhood at the time, but Sophia was typically gracious about this and made their new house welcoming. It was also convenient for Isambard, who was set to work on the tunnel – although not in the position he had hoped for. Marc had employed as Resident Engineer a 50-year-old Northumbrian engineer called William Armstrong. Isambard was merely Armstrong's assistant, along with three others: Richard Beamish, William Gravatt and Francis Riley.

Work began at the Rotherhithe side with the creation of a shaft down to the level of the tunnel, and the Brunels also had an innovative new method for this. Traditionally a hole would be dug down, and then lined with bricks. Instead, the Brunels built a brick tower, 42 feet high and 50 feet in diameter, and then – by digging within it – sunk it from the surface under its own 100-ton weight. By 6 June it had reached its full depth.[23] Now, the Great Shield – which had been constructed by Marc's partner Henry Maudsley – could be put in place.

Tunnelling began on 28 November 1825. From the start, work was slow. They had only gone 100 yards from the riverbank when the layer of clay, promised by the geologists, vanished. Now they were tunnelling through mud and soft soil. Yet, as soon as Marc discovered the difficulties, and attempted to tackle them, the Thames Tunnel Company turned up the pressure to compensate for lost time. They put the men on piecework in an attempt to increase productivity, and at the same time doubled the distance the boards were extended forward, against Marc's advice. Now the area of soil exposed was doubled – and so was the danger. Marc was fighting both the Thames Tunnel Company and the treacherous conditions.

The Thames in the 1820s was little more than an open sewer; the ground beneath it was putrid. The soil rotted away the men's fingernails and the stench in the air clogged their lungs. Besides the sickness this caused, the men were often drunk, in an effort to fog over and forget their disgusting place of work. But Isambard and his father mucked in, and toiled alongside the men in the tunnel.

In April 1826, the strain got to Armstrong; he broke and resigned. Isambard took over his responsibilities, along with Beamish, Gravatt and Riley. Shortly after, Marc became ill with pleurisy, an inflammation of the lungs. Although he slowly recovered, when he returned to work, much of his time was taken up at the surface with logistics and dealing with the difficult Board of Directors of the Thames Tunnel Company.

So, on 3 January 1827, Isambard Kingdom Brunel formally

Construction on the Thames Tunnel shows men at work in the tunnelling shield

took control as Resident Engineer of the Tunnel; Beamish, Gravatt and Riley were made his assistants. He was faced with the great responsibility of running the tunnel – at the age of only 21. It was a greater challenge than most have to face in their lifetime.

Throughout his childhood, Brunel's father, Marc, had primed him for success. Brunel was itching with ambition; he had already developed a fear and hatred of mediocrity. Now his talents – and his character – would be truly tested.

# The Thames Tunnel

Isambard Kingdom Brunel was an instant success as a leader of the tunnel works. He had incredible energy and maintained his vigorous manner on just a few hours sleep a night. He would work 12-hour shifts, six days a week, sometimes supervising the tunnelling for 36 hours at a stretch. By working alongside the men, Brunel showed he was far more than a mere administrator, but he made it clear that he was not one of them: he was their boss and he expected their hard work and their obedience. He lived the job of running the tunnel – he even made it his home, sharing a cabin with Gravatt near the tunnel mouth in Rotherhithe.

It was Brunel's job now to supervise and instruct the Somerset miners and Irish labourers working on the shield, and the brick-layers who lined the tunnel behind them. This was no easy task – the men had little training and were often drunk and unruly. While Armstrong might have put up with this, Brunel didn't. He sacked the drunks, and trained the remaining men and instilled discipline, getting them to line up at the mouth of the tunnel before starting work in the morning. Despite his youth, Brunel seemed to do this with a readily firm hand and some gusto.

On top of this, Brunel's job required keeping an eye on the quality of the bricks – if they weren't up to scratch they had to be sent back; he also had to check the engines pumping out the Thames water, and supervise the removal of the spoil from the tunnel.

Perhaps most difficult of all, he had to deal with the Directors of the Thames Tunnel Company. Opposition between the Brunels and the Directors grew daily: from the outset they prioritised profit above safety. Marc had designed a major drain to run below the tunnel that would allow any water that collected or flooded into the tunnel to run off safely, but the Directors refused it on the grounds of cost. In doing so, they got rid of Marc's 'safety valve' in the tunnel, so leaving all the men working inside it constantly vulnerable to flooding and even drowning.

The Directors chastised the Brunels for the slow pace of the tunnel's growth. On a good day, the tunnel would progress 3 feet in one day; but by early 1827 their average was only 13 feet in one

A cartoon depicts the Thames Tunnel being flooded

week.[24] Rising costs were also making the Directors concerned for their profits: in October 1826, 180 men were employed on the tunnel but that figure had increased to 467 by March 1827.[25]

In February 1827, with 300 feet of the archway completed, the chairman of the company, William Smith, imposed a plan which he thought might safeguard some of the profit: he opened the tunnel to the public. It cost a shilling to descend into the tunnel and watch the men at work on the giant shield. Hundreds of visitors, keen to see the technical marvel, massed into the tunnel every day and watched the digging from behind a barrier. For Brunel and his father, Marc, this was not just an extra burden – it was an unnecessary danger. The visitors were not only inhaling the stinking air in the tunnel, but also standing in the middle of an insecure structure that could collapse at any time.

The conditions got worse as the tunnel lengthened and air and light became even more scant. Fumes and gases carrying disease built up in the tunnel, as a result of the Directors limiting the expenditure on drainage and ventilation. In that same month, Assistant Engineer Riley caught river fever from the foul water and died. Soon after, Beamish succumbed to a serious illness that left him blind in one eye. Both were victims of the conditions in the tunnel.

The Brunels' concern about the safety of the tunnel grew. On 6 April, Marc wrote in his diary: 'We have no alternative but trusting the shield. The roof is nothing but loose sand. Awful!'[26] The situation can only have been made worse by the many false alarms sent up by the miners. The Irish labourers in particular could create waves of panic by their practice of turning out the lights 'in the old belief that under the cover of darkness the water could not find and overwhelm them'.[27] Marc was constantly nervous, convinced that it was just a matter of time before the tunnel gave in, on workers and visitors, who now numbered almost 600 a day.

They didn't have to wait long. At the end of April, bits of broken glass, china and old boots fell into the frame from the roof of the tunnel. This junk from the bottom of the Thames was a clear sign that they were tunnelling dangerously close to the riverbed – much closer than they had realised. Watermen working on the Thames told Marc that he was tunnelling into an underwater quarry, a section of the riverbed that had been dredged for gravel. If they continued digging into this quarry, the river would break in and flood the tunnel. Visitors continued to come to the tunnel; Isambard and his father Marc waited anxiously to see if it would collapse.

'Notwithstanding every prudence on our part, a disaster may still occur. May it not be when the arch is full of visitors! It is too awful to think of it. I have done my part by recommending to the directors to shut the tunnel. My solicitude is not lessened for that; I have, indeed, no rest, I may say I have had none for many weeks. So far the shield has triumphed over immense obstacles and it will carry the Tunnel through. During the preceding night, the whole of the ground over our heads must have been in movement, and that, too, at high water. The shield must, therefore, have supported upwards of Six hundred tons!'

Marc Brunel, diary, May 13th 1827.

On 18 May it happened. Beamish was on duty in the tunnel supervising 150 men, and had put on his sou'wester to prepare for the usual dripping into the tunnel. As the tide rose, the weight on the frames became unbearable and the river broke through. Beamish cried out for help. A great wave soared through the tunnel, carrying boxes and barrels and timbers. The noise was deafening. It knocked the men off their feet and smashed away the lower part of the access staircase. Gravatt and Isambard managed to pull several men out; incredibly, no one was killed.

Just 24 hours after the disaster, Isambard was back on site, trying to take stock of the damage. He borrowed a diving bell from the West India Dock Company to inspect the riverbed; like a giant hand bell, this was an open-ended device, which depended simply on the air pressure inside it to keep the water out. At the bottom of the river, he could see directly into the tunnel, and even stepped off the footboard of the diving bell and onto the frame of the shield.

During a second trip down in the diving bell, one of Isambard's assistants, Mr Pinckney, had been tempted to step onto the riverbed below but neglected to keep hold of the diving bell – he was only saved when Isambard had stuck out his leg for Pinckney to cling to.

Marc decided to plug the hole. This process took weeks – and 19,500 cubic yards of bagged clay. On 11 June, they were able to start pumping the water out of the tunnel, and making repairs.

The flooding of the Thames Tunnel

After a couple of days, 150 feet of the tunnel was clear, so Isambard decided to take a look. This time he took a boat, accompanied by several miners, wearing only bathing trunks. They punted along until they hit a big bank of silt, when Brunel was able to climb out onto the bank and into the frames. They were engulfed in mud but still intact.

For the fearless Isambard, this was all a great adventure, and his diary is crackling with excitement as he describes what happens:

*I wish I had kept this journal with me even at work on the river. What a dream it now appears to me. Going down in the Diving Bell, finding and examining the hole, standing on the corner of No12! The novelty of the thing, the excitement by the occasional risk attending our subaquatic excursion* [;] *the crowds of boats to witness our works . . . what sensations! . . . Standing on the arch – the engine rattling away – my father more cautious certainly foresaw the consequences of too quick a pumping – but we prevailed. NB never* <u>*will*</u> *I then be prevailed upon by others to do what I think imprudent.*[28]

It was 1 October before digging with the shield could begin again. All the time, their resources and energy were being used to repair the tunnel rather than extend it. But the filling of the hole was such an achievement that Isambard decided to mark it with a great banquet on Saturday 10 November, held in the tunnel. Fifty guests – the Directors and their friends – sat down to dinner in the West Arch, which was draped all in crimson, while they were accompanied by the band of the Coldstream Guards. Meanwhile, 120 miners ate beef and drank beer in the East Arch. Later in the evening, the men brought forward a present for Brunel: a pick and shovel, a sign of their recognition and appreciation of his leadership.

The celebrations over, they got back to work. But it wasn't long before the tunnel was once more in danger. On 2 January 1828, several rocks came in through the riverbed and fell into the frames of the shield. Brunel decided that this time they would not stop – if they tunnelled quickly they could get past the danger zone, and brick it up before it could collapse.[29] Water trickled through the frames and into the tunnel. Yet they carried on.

On 8 January, with the water still trickling in and digging still going ahead, Don Miguel, Pretender to the throne of

Portugal, came to see the shield with several other visitors. It was a nerve-wracking visit for Brunel who feared the half-built structure might squash this dignitary, but everyone left unscathed.

Four days later, at six in the morning, Beamish was above ground in the office while Brunel was working down on the frames with two miners called Collins and Ball. Suddenly a great column of water washed through the tunnel, blowing out the lights and knocking the men down. A great baulk of timber fell on top of Brunel's leg. He struggled to free himself in the darkness, but was immediately swept up on a great surge of water. The watchman and screaming miners had alerted Beamish who came rushing down the visitors' stairs – the workmen's stairs being packed with escaping miners. From the stairs Beamish saw Isambard Brunel floating towards him on a great surge of water – injured and unconscious but still breathing. Beamish grabbed him and pulled him out of the water.

Marc Brunel acknowledges the crowd's applause at the opening of the Thames Tunnel

If Beamish had been any later the great tide of water would have dragged Brunel with it, as it receded, with no chance of survival. Brunel's escape was extremely narrow. Others were not so lucky: six miners were killed, including Collins and Ball who were later found crushed beneath the wooden platform behind the shield used by the bricklayers.

Despite the trauma, once Brunel came round, he immediately set about tackling the situation, and assessing the damage. He refused to go home, and ordered the diving bell to be prepared. Since he couldn't walk, or get in the bell, he demanded instead to be taken onto the bell barge so that he could direct its lowering down into the Thames, refusing to leave until he knew the extent of the damage.[30]

Brunel wasn't aware of it, but the damage to his body was severe; in addition to the wound to his leg, he had sustained serious internal injuries. He spent a few days in bed, and then set off to Brighton to convalesce. But on 8 February he wrote in his diary: *Violent haemorrhage after riding horse.*[31] The bleeding continued, and so Beamish was sent to bring him back to London.

Brunel was too ill to return to work, so it was left to Marc to direct the clearing-out of the tunnel. This time, it took 4,500 tons of clay to block the hole. The cost of this was so great that there was not enough money for tunnelling to continue. In August 1828, the Directors ordered the tunnel to be bricked up. Negotiations continued, but

Work on the tunnel resumed in 1835, when the Treasury gave the Thames Tunnel Company a loan of £270,000. The tunnel was finished in March 1843 – but not to Marc's specifications. In the end there was not enough money to build slopes down to each entrance to allow vehicles to drive in and out. Instead, staircases were built, rendering it merely a novelty for pedestrians, until it became part of the London Underground in 1865. Marc Brunel was knighted for his work by Queen Victoria in 1841. Today his tunnel is an integral part of the East London line, connecting Rotherhithe and Wapping stations.

the tunnel remained closed. On 6 December 1831 Isambard wrote in his diary:

*Tunnel is now I think dead.*

*The commissioners have refused on the grounds of want of security – this is the first time I have felt able to cry at least for these 10 years. Some further attempts may be made – but – it will never be finished now in my father's lifetime I fear. However, nil desperandum has always been my motto – we may succeed yet. Perseverantia.*[32]

Marc had to endure his great project becoming the object of ridicule on the streets and in the newspapers, *The Times* having christened it 'the Great Bore'.

The flooding of the tunnel changed Brunel's life, projecting him into a bleak period lasting several years. He had just begun to taste the life of a successful engineer, and now it seemed he was rendered useless. He fell into a period of depression. The only big project that he had worked on had just failed, and with neither experience nor reputation there seemed to be no hope of another. It seemed that his father's aspirations, and his own hard work, were to no avail.

# From the Doldrums to Clifton Bridge

After the collapse of the tunnel in January 1828, Brunel was left without a project. Before he could find another, he had to first recover his health, so he returned to Brighton to convalesce. Unfortunately, his injuries were serious and it took over six months for them to heal. So began a frustrating and introspective period for Brunel, lasting several years. He felt wracked by anxieties over what he perceived to be a depressing lack of progress in his career, and he privately pondered and questioned his feelings in his diaries.

Encouraged by his father, he had already begun two diaries, his Private Diary and his Thames Tunnel Diary; both primarily concerned with work. But in October 1827 – a few months before the collapse of the tunnel – Brunel had begun a new Personal Diary, in which he recorded his innermost anxieties and ambitions. Fiercely guarded about his emotions, he kept it padlocked and carefully hidden.

Although this was by far the slimmest of Brunel's diaries, it is also by far the most revealing. From the beginning, it is open and self-critical. It shows a person who is domineering – yet aware of that.

*When thinking of this journal whole volumes crowded on me . . . Now I am quite without an idea. As to my character? . . . My self conceit and love of glory or rather approbation vie with each other which shall govern me. The latter is so strong that even of a dark night riding home when I pass some unknown person who perhaps does not even look at me I catch myself trying to look big on my little pony. The former on reflection does not seem to counteract the latter. I often do the most silly useless things to appear to advantage before or attract the attention of thou . . . The former renders me domineering intolerant nay even quarrelsome with those who do not flatter me.*[33]

But the journal also reveals that – at the age of 22 – Brunel is preoccupied with women and the possibility of marriage.

*As long as health continues, one's prospects tolerable, and present efforts whatever they may be tolerably successful, then indeed a bachelor life is luxurious . . . What independence! For one who's (sic) ambition is to distinguish himself in the eyes of the public such a feeling of comfort is almost indispensable. But on the other hand, in sickness or in disappointment how delightfull (sic) to have a companion whose sympathy one is sure of.*[34]

Brunel was a sociable and confident person. And this diary reveals that at the age of 21 he had already embarked on several relationships – the most important with "E.H.", Ellen Hume, the daughter of family friends in Manchester.

*. . . I have had as I suppose most men have had numerous <u>attachments</u> if they deserve the name and each in its turn has appeared to me <u>the true one</u>. EH ___ is the oldest and most constant now however gone by. During her reign\* – several inferior ones caught my attention.*

*\*nearly seven years!!!*

*I need hardly remind myself of ??D.C___ and O.S ___ and numerous others. With E Hume it was mutual and I trust the present feeling is also mutual in this case. The sofa scenes must appear now to her as to me rather ridiculous. She was a nice girl and had she improved as a girl of her age ought to have done.* [Rest of page cut out.][35]

When and why Brunel made the censorious cut to this page is not known – leaving the intriguing question of what exactly he was trying to erase, or hide from himself. But in the last sentence there is the beginnings of a somewhat pompous judgement of Ellen – perhaps he carried this too far, even in his own opinion.

He goes on to toy with the idea of proposing to Ellen – as long as she comes up to scratch.

*I have written a long letter yesterday – her answer shall decide. If she wavers I <u>ought</u> to break off for I cannot hope to be in a condition to marry her and to continue in this state of suspense is wronging her after all. I shall most likely remain a bachelor and that I think is best for me . . . my profession is after all my only fit wife . . . Oh Ellen Ellen if you have kept up your musick and can even play only tolerably we might be very happy yet . . .* (sic)

Even now, at the moment of proposal, Brunel's desperate ambition creeps in and interferes, and he is a mass of confusions, torn between his career and marriage – convinced that marriage should have some tangible benefit to offer to him. Two months later, in August 1828, the concern for his career seems to be winning the internal battle of Brunel's concerns and he writes that: *I am half afraid of my old attachment binding me and yet have not the heart to break it off.*

With what seems like pure iron discipline, Brunel turns his focus to his work at the time – continuing with the Gaz experiments, and searching for work as an engineer. But tellingly, the diary contains no account of Ellen's response to Brunel's proposal. It is hard to tell whether he chooses work of free will or if Ellen made that choice for him.

*What a life – the life of a dreamer – am always building castles in the air what time I waste – I have refrained from several indulgences by making up my mind and thus making a sort of vow . . . I have had long correspondence with Ellen which I think I managed well, I may now consider myself independent.*[36]

The career wins out. And throughout the diary, Brunel's chief concern in this diary is – as ever – anxiety over his future prospects.

*My ambition or whatever it may be called (it is not the mere wish to be rich) is rather extensive but still I am not afraid that I shall be unhappy if I do not reach the rank of hero and commander in chief of his majesty's forces . . . In the steam (gas) boat department – this is rather a favourite castle in the air of mine. Make the gas engine answer fit out some vessels (of course a war) take some prizes nay some island or fortified tower, get employed by government . . . construct and command a fine fleet of them and fight fight – in fact take Algiers or something in that style. Build a splendid manufactory for gas engines . . . a yard for building the boats . . . at last be rich enough to have a house built of which I have even made the drawings &c. Be the first Engineer and an example to future ones.* [37]

He calls his dreams his 'chateaux d'Espagne', his term for castles in the sky, and they re-appear in all his diaries. A month later he is even more anxious about his future, and concerned that he might be under-achieving

*What will become of me? . . . Eh? Mr Pitt was only 22 Prime Minister and for the first time in his life!!! I may be said to have almost built this tunnel having been active Resident Engineer. What Castles!! My gas engine – a tunnel – tunnels – what a field. Yet I may miss it.* [38]

And by the summer of 1828, after the demise of the tunnel, Brunel is comparing himself, unfavourably, with his rivals.

*The young Rennies whatever their real merit will have built London Bridge the finest bridge in Europe – and have such a connection with government as to defy competition. Palmer has built London Docks . . . and established a connection which ensures his fortune. While I shall have been engaged in the Tunnel which failed – which was abandoned – a pretty recommendation . . .* [39]

But in 1829, Brunel finally got his chance. In Bristol, a competition was announced for the design of a bridge to cross the Avon Gorge, connecting Leigh Woods on one side with Clifton on the other.[40] At the time, this sheer drop of 250 feet could only be crossed by a slipway, by a long detour in a rowing boat, or more dangerously, by being hauled across the gap in a basket suspended from a wrought iron bar (the basket was a fashionable place for proposals at the time).

The challenge attracted some of the greatest engineers of the age. Brunel was not to be left out and went at once to Bristol.[41]

Brunel had no specialist knowledge of suspension bridges but, with the help of his father Marc, he drew up four designs, offering the committee a choice of different sites for the bridge.

An artist's impression of the proposed Clifton Bridge

Each of Brunel's designs was daring, with spans ranging from 870 to 916 feet – the latter being the longest suspension bridge that had ever been proposed. He submitted his plans as beautiful sepia drawings on the 19 November 1829, alongside 22 other entries. From these, a shortlist was drawn up: Brunel and four other entrants were on it. Thomas Telford, designer of the Menai Suspension Bridge[42] and then president of the Institution of Civil Engineers, was to choose the winner.

But Telford did no such thing. Instead he announced that none of the submitted designs was acceptable. Having built the Menai with a central span of 580 feet, he was convinced from the experience of seeing it swing in gales that 600 feet was the maximum possible span that could provide enough lateral resistance to the wind. He rejected Brunel's longer-spanned bridges out of hand. And, having rejected all the other entrants too, Telford proffered his own design instead.

Telford proposed that two enormous Gothic towers be built up from the bottom of the gorge, so creating three shorter spans, instead of one big one. Fizzing with injustice, Brunel wrote to the Bridge Committee. Not only had Telford failed to see that Brunel's calculations were correct, but his own design of two incredibly tall towers would surely sink into the soft ground below.

Fortunately for Brunel, Telford's plan was also extremely expensive and when, in 1830, there were still insufficient funds to build it, it was dropped and the competition was opened again. A second adjudicator, the scientist Davies Gilbert, was appointed in Telford's place. This time, Brunel submitted a single, new design for a bridge – but he compromised his original designs by adding a large abutment on the Leigh Woods side of the river, so reducing the overall span to 630 feet. In engineering terms, this compromise was unnecessary – but it placated the judges. Telford submitted the same plan as before.

Having submitted his plan, Brunel returned to London to work on another project. He had a won a small commission from Sir James South, to build an observatory at South's home in Kensington. Brunel took the dimensions on 5 October 1830, and commenced on the plans. The following spring, the Observatory was finished, replete with a fully revolving dome, bisected by a telescope slot that could be covered with mechanically-operated shutters.

On 20 May 1831, South held a celebratory opening with Brunel as guest of honour. But, on receiving a bill which exceeded Brunel's original estimates, South quickly turned on him. Not only did South refuse to pay, but shortly afterwards an anonymous article was published by the Athenaeum written, or at least informed, by South in which the observatory was described as 'an

The Clifton Suspension Bridge as it is today

absurd project [which] had no other object than the display of a tour de force, and was an effort to produce effect on the part of the architect'.[43] Brunel was deeply hurt by this, and pasted the full article into his diary. He considered libel action, and consulted his good friend Charles Babbage (inventor of the progenitor computer, the 'difference engine') who advised that Brunel should write to the Editor at the Athenaeum[44] but in the end Brunel did neither – he was, after all, just a junior engineer.

While the Observatory debacle was unfolding, the results of the second Clifton bridge competition were announced. Once again, Brunel found himself passed over in favour of one W Hawks.[45] This time, Brunel wasn't taking no for an answer. He was already acquainted with Davies Gilbert from the scientific community in London, and on 17 March, Brunel went to Bristol, to confront Gilbert, who (along with his assistant the marine engineer John Seaward) had criticised the chains and anchorage in Brunel's design. Brunel arranged a meeting with Gilbert and the other judges to argue the case for his design. It worked – and Brunel was declared the winner.

On 27 March 1831, Brunel wrote to Ben Hawes excitedly telling him of his successful persuasion: *I have to say that of all the wonderful feats I have performed since I have been in this part of the world, I think yesterday I performed the most wonderful. I produced unanimity amongst fifteen men who were all quarrelling about the most ticklish subject – taste.*[46]

At the age of 24, this was a great achievement but can't have made him popular among older Engineers – especially Telford, who wasn't even among the finalists this time.

This was Brunel's first successful design, and it displayed the aesthetic flair and daring that would make him famous. There was an interest for things Egyptian at the time – fuelled by stories from people taking their Grand Tours, and by Napoleon's ill-fated campaign in Egypt (from 1798 to 1801). And so, Brunel adorned the towers of his design with images of sphinxes and hieroglyphics. He even intended to pay homage to the bridge itself, in a series of giant panels depicting its construction.

Only a fraction of this design is visible today in the finished bridge. The exotic sphinxes, and the hieroglyphs are missing. There is no sign of the panels depicting the bridge's construction. Although the shape of the towers remains as Brunel designed them, the final bridge was modified from Brunel's plans; Brunel would not live to see this bridge – his first success – completed.

Work had started quickly on the bridge – there was an opening ceremony on 21 July 1831. This was a chance for Brunel to show off and enjoy praise. Cannons were fired, flags were raised and bands played. Sir Abraham Elton led the celebrations and said of Brunel 'The time will come when as that gentleman walks along the street, or passes from city to city, the cry would be raised "There goes the man who reared that stupendous work, the ornament of Bristol and the wonder of the age"'.[47]

In the summer of 1831 – after five years of anxiety, soul-searching and hard work – it seemed like nothing could now stop Isambard Kingdom Brunel. He had forsaken his dalliances with marriage and had chosen instead those 'chateaux d'Espagnes' which were filled with accomplishment; at last he was on his way to becoming an engineer. It seemed that his fortunes had changed, and nothing now could stand in the way of his success.

# Bristol

With the commencement of work on the Clifton Suspension Bridge, Brunel seemed set on the road to independence and success as an Engineer at last. Most importantly, the Clifton Bridge had brought him to Bristol, the city where he would find great success and great allies.

But no sooner had work begun on the bridge, than it hit financial and legal problems – funds were insufficient and the approach on the Leigh Woods side was disputed. In autumn 1831, things got even worse when the city of Bristol was paralysed by riots.

The Bristol Riots were sparked by the ongoing struggle for Parliamentary Reform. In November 1830, the new Whig Prime Minister, Earl Grey, announced to King William IV that he intended to reform Parliament by giving the vote to growing cities such as Manchester, Birmingham and Leeds, and getting rid of 'rotten boroughs', where votes could be bought. On 22 September 1831, the House of Commons passed the Reform Bill, only for the House of Lords to overturn it. Riots flared up across England, but none were as fierce as those in Bristol.

The Riots lasted three days, from 29 to 31 October 1831; Brunel was staying in Clifton at the time, and witnessed some of the action. Feeling for the Reform Bill was particularly strong in Bristol, since although the city had representation in Parliament, in 1830 it had just 6,000 votes for 104,000 people. This corruption created a strong feeling of resentment, and the city was like a dry tinderbox ready to be sparked into violence.

When the Reform Bill was put to Parliament, and subsequently denounced by the House of Lords, one of the members who spoke most strongly against it was Sir Charles Wetherall, Tory Magistrate of Bristol.

On 29 October, Wetherall rode into Bristol to open the Assize Courts; it was more than the people of Bristol could bear. He was pelted with stones, and chased by a furious mob to Charles Square, where he took refuge in the Mansion House. City authorities called in military aid: the hated Dragoons. Although their leader, Colonel Brereton, read the Riot Act, he refused to open fire or disperse the mob. The chaos continued.

The next day there was a fresh attack; Colonel Brereton asked the rioters to disperse and then withdrew his troops. But the mob took over the city and proceeded to set fire to the Mansion and the Custom Houses, the Bishop's Palace and much of Queen's Square. They broke into three gaols and freed the prisoners, before setting fire to those buildings too.

It was at this point that Brunel joined the fray. He met up with Nicholas Roche, one of the judges on the Clifton Bridge committee, and together they were sworn in as Special Constables, 'pro-establishment' members of the public drafted in to boost police numbers. In this instance, Brunel was firmly on the side of authority and the establishment. (This was not an ardent political stance however, and in other occasions his views and actions were quite liberal.)

Seeing the city in uproar, Brunel acted to save some of it. He rushed in to the Mansion House, scooped up pictures and a plate and – armed only with the back of a broken chair – fought his way to secure them at the Customs House. He even arrested a looter, who would have been hanged for his crimes had he not struggled free from Brunel's grasp.

Finally at 5am the next morning, Brereton returned with his troops, and finally succeeded in dispersing the mob.

In the aftermath of the riots, both the mayor and the Corporation of Bristol were prosecuted for failing to defend the city, but the mayor was acquitted and the prosecutions dropped. Four rioters were hung for their actions; many more were flogged. Colonel Brereton was court-martialled for negligence, and Brunel was called as a witness. But Brereton shot himself through the heart before he could be sentenced.

A cartoon depicts the rioting crowds in Queen's Square, Bristol, 1830

The riots finally put paid to any progress on Brunel's suspension bridge. Once more, he was left without work or prospects. But this time, there was a difference – a shred of hope. Although he didn't know it yet, Brunel had already made the most important contact of his career – with the city of Bristol. This connection would eventually prove to be the cornerstone of his career, but in the meantime, he faced a struggle. Once again, he fell into a period of frustration and anxiety. As Brunel looked for work with little luck, he grew increasingly despondent.

He went back to his work on the Gaz experiments. But after months of time and effort, there was still little progress and, inevitably, disappointment. Finally, he was forced to admit defeat and abandoned the Gaz engine altogether.

*Gaz – after a number of experiments I fear we must come to the conclusion that (with carbonic acid at least) no efficient advantage on the score of economy of fuel can be obtained. All the time and expense both enormous devoted to this thing for nearly 10 years are therefore wasted.*[48]

Brunel travelled the country, trying to win work, but with little success. In November 1831, he finally won a commission to design a complex of docks for the River Wear in Sunderland, to accommodate the growing export of coal from the nearby collieries. He chose a site at Monkwearmouth and travelled up to Sunderland by carriage, and then took the long, picturesque route home. He saw Newcastle, Durham Cathedral and then Manchester, where he visited friends, the Hulme family. And while in Manchester, on 5 December, he took a fateful trip on the Liverpool & Manchester Railway, which had opened just the year before. Brunel was immediately inspired, it seems, and immediately alive to the possibilities for improvement – he wrote in his diary while the train was moving, to record its shakiness:

*I record this specimen of the shaking on the Manchester Railway – the time is not far off when we shall be able to take our coffee and write while going, noiseless and smoothly, at 45 miles per hour – let me try.*[49]

(Since Brunel's writing at this point isn't actually too bad, it's possible that he simply fell in love with the railways, at once.) But the prospect of Brunel becoming an engineer on the railways was a far-off dream. He was still a very junior engineer, with little more than a failed tunnel, a publicly-maligned observatory and an abandoned bridge to his name. He returned to London and drew up his plans for the Monkwearmouth docks. But they were rejected by Parliament as too expensive. He applied for a post as an engineer on the Newcastle & Carlisle Railway but was, once more, rejected.

Brunel's growing self-doubt and despondency is all-too evident in the last entry to his Personal Diary, made on 2 August 1832. He writes an inscription to his brother-in-law Ben Hawes, to whom he (somewhat melodramatically) wills the diary:

*I always anticipated pleasure and perhaps instruction in reading over this my journal . . . Ben I have a painful conviction that I am fast becoming a selfish cold-hearted ambitious brute – only you don't see it . . . I'm unhappy – exceedingly so. How convenient the excitement of this election came just in time to conceal it.*[50]

These were the elections of September 1832, held after the Reform Act was finally passed by both Houses of Parliament. Ben Hawes stood for the seat in Lambeth as the Liberal candidate; this was an opportunity for Brunel to support him and, moreover, to keep himself busy. For Ben, it was a successful campaign and for Brunel it was a distraction; one of the few political occasions he ever involved himself with. (And this time, he was on the side of the Liberals.)

Just at this time, Brunel's fortunes began to turn. His acquaintance with the city of Bristol was about to start to pay dividends. Late in the summer of 1832, his former ally Nicholas Roche – a trustee of the Clifton Bridge – used his influence as a member of the Dock Committee to get Brunel a commission from the Dock Company to report on the condition of the Floating Harbour.

The Floating Harbour had been built in between 1803 and 1809, and its antiquated state was somewhat symbolic of Bristol's fortunes as a city. It was constructed to address the problem of ships being stranded twice a day when the water drained out of the tidal rivers that ran through Bristol: the Frome and the Avon. By shutting off a loop in the River Avon, an enclosed wet dock was created which always had enough depth to float a ship – hence the name, the Floating Harbour. The Avon itself was diverted into a new tidal cut. When Brunel arrived in Bristol, the harbour was in need of updating – it was silted up and filled with sewage twice a day. On top of this, the builders of the Floating Harbour had not anticipated the growth in merchant shipping, and the harbour was simply too small.

The fortunes of the city of Bristol – which to a large degree were dependent on the harbour – were in decline. For several centuries, Bristol had been the major port of the west, the second port of England, but now that honour fell to Liverpool, where large, enclosed wet docks had been built, allowing access to the Atlantic and the lucrative trade in African slaves, as well as tobacco and sugar. Bristol simply hadn't kept up.

Brunel examined the Harbour and in August 1832 submitted his report. His solution was based on the water supply: at the moment the water was stagnant, but he realised that it must be kept moving to carry both the silt and the effluent away. He recommended that the height of the Netham Dam (which fed the water into the harbour) be raised, to increase the flow of water through the harbour, and suggested that the dam be converted from an overfall weir to an underfall weir, by putting sluices at the bottom end of the harbour so that any silt would be dragged out when the tide fell. As a more immediate and short-term measure, he also recommended the use of a dragboat to remove the current build-up of mud.

But the ever short-sighted Directors of the Dock Company wanted to save money, and took only a couple of Brunel's recommendations on board: the addition of the sluices to convert the dam to an underfall weir, and the removal of the mud with a dragboat.

When even this small part of the work was complete, the improvement in the Harbour was immediately evident. (Brunel was asked to examine the Harbour once again in 1842, and this time he insisted on the raising of the Netham Dam.)

The riverfront and docks at Bristol. The spires of St Stepney, St Augustine and the Cathe

visible. 1830

Nicholas Roche was impressed by Brunel's work and soon presented him with another opportunity in Bristol – one that would transform Brunel's life. This time, Roche brought Brunel the chance to work on the railways.

Since the summer of 1832, a plan was being hatched in Bristol of which Brunel knew nothing – the idea was for a railway that would run from Bristol to London. After all, a London to Birmingham line had been approved, and a Manchester to Warrington line had opened in 1830. Railways were coming along at a great rate. The idea of a London to Bristol line had been mooted several times since 1824,[51] but it was only in the autumn of 1832 that a committee of four men gathered with serious intent: John Harford, George Jones, William Tothill and Thomas Guppy. In the spring of 1833 they got the backing of Bristol's power-holders: the Merchant Venturers; Bristol Corporation; the Dock Company amongst others. Next, they needed an Engineer.

Roche took the idea to Brunel who was, of course, extremely excited by it. That night, 21 February 1833, Brunel marked this great new opportunity in his diary simply as: *B.R.* (Bristol Railway), adding *How will this end.*[52]

There was no guarantee that Brunel would be Engineer to the line. He would have to compete against others for the contract to build the railway: the applicants would survey the line, and the winner would be the one with the lowest estimate. This enraged Brunel, who believed the contract should not simply be awarded on the basis of cost, and he wrote to the committee stating:

*You are simply giving a premium to the man who makes the most flattering promises. The route I will survey will not be the cheapest – but it will be the best.*[53]

He left the committee to ponder this, while he travelled back to London to attend the annual meeting of the Thames Tunnel Company. He returned two days later on 6 March, to discover that the committee had confirmed his appointment. This, however, gave Brunel a new cause for complaint; he was expected to work "in conjunction with"[54] William Townsend, a man for whom Brunel had no respect whatsoever. Townsend was a local man, and although he already surveyed the Bristol & Gloucestershire Railway, this was a very small horse-drawn tramway between two local coalmines, and it didn't impress Brunel. On 22 February 1833 Brunel wrote in his diary:

> . . . *although I had no wish to be otherwise than as gentlemen perfectly on an equality yet as our standing I would distinguish us by his generally having acted as Surveyor, I as Engineer, then there would be no fear of our interests clashing and throughout we would pull together . . . how the devil am I to get on with him tied to my neck I know not.*[55]

The preliminary survey was extremely hard work – it meant covering hundreds of miles of uneven ground on horseback, as Brunel and Townsend measured the ground and took levels to calculate their preferred route. In addition to this, they had to begin the job of persuading the owners of the land they surveyed to sell it to them – a difficult task since many of them were opposed to the railways, especially when they passed through their own property. For these enormous tasks Brunel and Townsend had just ten weeks. For the most part, Brunel left the unfortunate Townsend in the London office while he ventured out.

Once the survey was complete, the project was publicly launched on 30 July 1833. It was decided that there should also be a London committee, and that there should be 12 directors in each city. The first joint meeting of these two committees was held on 22 August at Lime Street in London. Brunel was rather disappointed by the lacklustre attitude of the directors: their lack of vigour and enthusiasm. There was some temerity about the project – it was after all an enormous undertaking, and at more than 100 miles, the longest stretch of railway yet proposed. But on 27 August, when the committee met again, Brunel was heartened by the more vigorous approach of Charles Saunders, secretary to the London committee. Brunel pronounced Saunders *an agreeable man*[56] and the two became great friends. It was at this meeting that Brunel was confirmed as the Engineer of the line, and the project was formally named; that night in his diary Brunel wrote the letters that would now dominate his life: 'GWR', Great Western Railway.

Brunel's Elizabethan hammerbeam roof and colonnade at the GWR Station at Temple Meads in Bristol

With his newfound status as Engineer of a major project, Brunel decided to upgrade his housing accordingly. He moved out from his parents' home and offices, and rented an office at 53 Parliament Street. He hired draughtsmen and a chief clerk called Joseph Bennett (who would stay with Brunel for 26 years). And since he would have to continue his relentless journeys between Bristol and London, Brunel ordered a carriage to be made. This four-horse britshcka became a mobile office containing a drawing board, his surveying equipment, a bed and a large supply of cigars, which he was now smoking almost constantly. It was soon nicknamed 'the Flying Hearse'.

On 7 September there was another meeting of the committee, when it was decided that Brunel should proceed with the detailed survey of the line. This meant the exhausting process of measuring the ground from Bristol to London had to be repeated, but this time more accurately. Brunel employed more assistants (in addition to Townsend) and spent his time studying plans and estimates, and trying to charm landowners into parting with their land. It was gruelling work and Brunel wrote to his assistant Hammond: *It is harder work than I like . . . I am rarely under twenty hours a day at it.*[57]

While Brunel worked on the survey, the company's directors tried to raise funds and support for the project – they must propose their railway in a Bill before Parliament, and for that they needed to raise half of the capital required to build the railway. For Brunel's 116-mile line, the total estimated cost was a whopping £3,000,000. Charles Saunders in particular travelled the West of England, trying to sell as many shares as possible at £100 each.

By the autumn of 1833 it was clear that the money raised was simply not enough. But if they waited for more funds, they would miss the upcoming Parliamentary session. So, on 18 October 1833 the Committee took a drastic measure. They would propose to Parliament just two short sections of the line: the end sections from Bristol to Bath, and from Reading to London, with the intention of raising the money for the remaining connecting section by the next Parliamentary session.

The Bill was finally submitted to Parliament in November 1833, and after a second reading on 16 April 1834 it was passed to committee stage for scrutiny in the House of Commons. Experts – the great and the good of railway engineering – were called to give evidence over the course of 56 days.

Opposition came from many landowners, including one farmer who claimed his cows would be killed passing under a railway bridge, and from other railway companies, such as the London & Southampton Railway who had submitted a Bill to Parliament in the same session. While the town of Windsor complained that the proposed line didn't come close enough, Eton College complained that it came far too near, and endangered the morality of its boys by making the (fallen) women of London far too accessible.

The main advocate for the line was Brunel, who stood in the witness box for 11 days. He was cross-examined by a Sergeant Mereweather, who tore at him viciously. But Brunel not only withstood the attack, he flourished under it. He revelled in the opportunity to display his knowledge, authority and wit to his Parliamentary audience. He made it a show, and of course he was the star.

During the hearing Brunel was concerned that his legal advisor, St George Burke, would wake up in time for the hearing each morning. Brunel came up with a solution. Since they were staying on the same street, Brunel hung some string between their apartments. In the mornings, he would pull the string, a bell would ring and Burke was awake. Brunel, of course, needed no such device – he never seemed to sleep.

Despite Brunel's stunning performance the GWR was still blocked. In particular there was great objection to the proposed terminus at Vauxhall, by the local residents. And, beyond that, a railway line consisting of just two end sections was an easy target; one opponent of the project called it 'neither "Great" nor "Western" nor a "Railway" at all but a gross deception, a trick, and a fraud upon the public in name, in title, and in substance'.[58] On 25 July 1834, the Bill was thrown out by the House of Lords.

Brunel and his colleagues took the Bill away to revise it. The main intention was to change the terminus, but Brunel had another concern. He had already noticed that the carriages built

A lithograph of entrants in the Rainhill Locomotive Steam Engine contest. Stephenson's Rocket (top) was the winner

by George Stephenson (used on the Stockton & Darlington Railway, and others) produced a swaying motion due to their narrow width, and short wheel base; Stephenson simply having adopted the 'coal-cart' gauge of 4 feet 8½ inches used at Killingworth Colliery where he built his first steam locomotive.[59]

While the GWR Bills were passed to and from Parliament, Brunel had time to consider Stephenson's gauge. He believed that he could make a smoother, more stable – and therefore much faster – ride by using a wide gauge of between 6 feet 10 inches and 7 feet. By placing the carriages between the rails, rather than over them, he reasoned he could lower the centre of gravity, and so reduce friction. This system would also allow larger-diameter wheels to be used, which would reduce friction even further. Speed would be paramount.

Brunel seized his chance to create a railway of entirely new dimensions. The first Bill contained a clause stipulating the narrow gauge in current usage, so before the second Bill was put before Parliament Brunel approached Lord Shaftesbury (who was responsible for drafting Bills) and asked him to remove it.

By February 1835, Saunders announced that £2,000,000 capital had been raised; now the GWR could return to Parliament with the revised Bill and a new terminus: they would end the line at Euston, by joining up with the London & Birmingham line near Queen's Park Station, northwest of the city.

This time, however, there was more serious opposition from the London & Southampton Railway which, having proposed a rival scheme, drew attention away from any possible flaws in their own plans by attacking the most ambitious part of Brunel's line: the Box Tunnel. Faced with hills to the east of Bath, Brunel had decided to go straight through them rather than round them. At more than one and three-quarter miles long, and with a gradient of 1 in 100 (going from the east side to the west), to be cut through the solid rock at the village of Box, it was a goldmine of potential problems for them to pick at. They called as a witness Dr Dionysius Lardner.

Lardner was Professor of Natural Philosophy and Astronomy at London University, but this didn't seem to prevent him from coming up with the most illogical and bizarre calculations. He contrived a calculation that apparently proved that if the brakes failed as a train entered the Box Tunnel, then due to the falling gradient it would gather speed and emerge at the other end at a speed of 120 mph. At this speed, he argued, any passenger would be suffocated as the pressure would be too great for them to breathe.

Brunel managed to counter Lardner's wild claims with his own calculations, and at last the Bill was passed. On 31 August 1835, the GWR was given Royal Assent from William IV – complete with the licence for Brunel to create a completely new design for railway lines and carriages.

The first time the directors heard anything of Brunel's rather momentous plans to revise the gauge was in a report submitted to them on 15 September 1835. Brunel argued his case and – almost entirely through the force of his personality – he won over the directors. He dismissed the objection of break of gauge at the junction with the Birmingham line as minor, believing it could be fixed with only an additional rail to create a mixed gauge at that point. The directors granted their backing for the broad gauge on 29 October 1835 (although this was not publicised until the next half-yearly shareholders meeting in August 1836). Now Brunel was free to create his broad-gauge system.

In December 1835, the railway started to take shape as we know it today, when GWR Directors abandoned the Euston terminus in favour of a new one at Paddington. The choice wasn't entirely their own: Stephenson and the London & Birmingham Railway were none too keen on sharing Euston with the GWR, especially in its broad gauge form. So a series of temporary platforms and wooden sheds were created at Paddington instead – the first version of the station.

Soon after, on Boxing Day night, 1835, Brunel sat down to add up his achievements, with a sense of great self-satisfaction. Now, he had good reason to be pleased with himself, for some of his abandoned works had also picked up:

An early view of Paddington Station

*The railway is now in progress. I am their Engineer to the finest work in England – a handsome salary – £2000 a year – on excellent terms with my Directors and all going smoothly, but what a fight we have had . . . it is like looking back on a fearful pass – but we have succeeded and it's not this alone but everything I have been engaged in has been successful . . .*[60]

Work had resumed on Clifton Bridge, Brunel's revised plans for the Monkwearmouth Docks at Sunderland had been passed by Parliament and their construction was underway, and work on the Thames Tunnel had resumed in March 1835 (under Marc Brunel's direction), the Thames Tunnel Company having secured a loan of £270,000 from the Government.

Best of all, the Great Western Railway was underway, and that had brought work on other lines (the Cheltenham; Bristol & Exeter; the Newbury branch; and the Bristol & Gloster (sic)) that were quickly growing out from the GWR. Finally, Brunel added up the capital invested in all this work, reaching a grand total of £5,320,000, *a pretty considerable capital to pass through my hands and this at the age of 29 – faith, not so young as I always fancy tho' I can hardly believe it when I think of it.* He concluded: *I have a cab and a horse – I have a secretary – in fact I am now a somebody. Everything has prospered . . . I don't like it, it can't last, bad weather must surely come.*[61]

And in this final premonition, he was right. Because, although he had lately achieved great success – in the city of Bristol – he had also seeded a problem. Somewhat quietly, he had ushered in the broad gauge railway. It was a move that would make life difficult not just for Brunel, but would have ramifications for thousands of people, and divide the field of engineering.

# Friendship and Marriage

For almost ten years now, since construction began on the Thames tunnel, Brunel had been consumed by work. But he had fantastic energy and a winning personality, and always made sure he had some fun and something of a social life. During these years, he had made important friendships and alliances through his work, particularly in Bristol. His Bristol friend Nicholas Roche, for example, had already played an important part in getting him work at the Bristol Docks and GWR. Besides his own strength of mind, these friends would prove to be perhaps Brunel's greatest resource in the tough years ahead.

While at the Docks, Brunel had met and earned the respect of another steadfast man, Captain Christopher Claxton, the Quay Warden. Claxton had served as a naval officer and was 16 years older than Brunel but they developed a strong friendship. When, years later, Brunel turned his hand to designing ships, Claxton would become his business partner – and would one day even save Brunel's life.

At Brunel's latest project in Bristol, the GWR, he met another of the greatest influences on his life: Thomas Guppy. Guppy would prove to be an invaluable friend and ally in the difficult times that lay ahead in the growth of the GWR. Like Brunel, Guppy had trained as an engineer. He served his apprenticeship at the great firm of Maudsley, Sons & Field and now ran a successful sugar-refining business with his brother, in Bristol. Guppy was a member of the original GWR committee who selected Brunel as their Engineer; he had an adventurous mind and would continue to back Brunel during his increasingly ambitious forays into the building of railways and ships.

These were the friends who would stand by Brunel in the difficult times ahead. But Brunel also made friends amongst the scientists and engineers with whom he mixed in London, where he liked to keep up with the latest research. In 1829, he became a member of the Institution of Civil Engineers; he attended lectures at the Royal Society with his father regularly (there are frequent records of this is his diary); in 1830 he was elected a Fellow. Amongst the friends he made here were Charles Babbage and Michael Faraday.

An engraving of Michael Faraday lecturing at The Royal Society

On the subject of romance, Brunel's diaries are rather quiet, after the days of the tunnel and his love for Ellen Hume. But in the summer of 1832, that all changed, thanks to Brunel's brother-in-law and old friend, Ben Hawes. On one of their many outings together, Ben took Brunel on a social visit to the house of another family – the Horsleys. And it was there that Brunel met his future wife. On 10 June 1832, Brunel makes a passing reference: *After lunch I went to Kensington – called on the Horsleys.* But this glancing mention represented a significant new stage in Brunel's life, as he spent more and more of his time with the Horsley family – or more specifically, their daughter Mary.

The Horsleys lived at No 1, High Row Kensington Gravel Pits (later 128 Church Street). They were a very creative family, whose lives were full of music and performance. William Horsley was a music teacher, and also a composer, who had married Elizabeth Callcott – the daughter of his tutor in vocal composition at Oxford.[62]

They had five children who all demonstrated artistic and musical talent. Their son John Horsley would one day become a well-known painter, and a member of the Royal Academy. When Brunel met him in 1832, he was still an art student and the two of them became great friends. Of their other children, Fanny was a talented artist (who would die young); Charles was studying music; Sophy, the youngest, was a brilliant pianist. But of greatest interest to Brunel was Mary, who at the age of 19 was the eldest, and who was the most beautiful in the family – although the least talented – and by all accounts the least warm.

Besides going out to see concerts, the Horsleys would put on productions of their own at home – pantomimes, concerts and plays – involving their family and friends. And they got an amazing audience – the great and the good of the music world were recorded in Sophy's tiny autograph album, including Felix Mendelssohn, a frequent visitor to the house.[63]

Brunel was happy to be drawn into these productions – and his showmanship found a vent on their home stage. The Horsleys' liveliness must have seemed incredibly attractive to Brunel, who had spent so much of his time holed up in his deathly dark britshcka, with his unforgiving calculations and exhausting petitions for land.

Having met the Horsleys in 1832, there follows an ongoing stream of references in Brunel's diaries to visits to their household, and to attending concerts with them. Brunel and Mary grew increasingly close.

In 1836, Brunel decided to act on his feelings. On 14 April that year, he worked through his achievements in his diary. Not only was the GWR going ahead, but he was being recruited as the Engineer for other adjoining lines. He wrote in his diary:

*I have added to my stock in trade the Plymouth Railway, the Oxford branch and today somewhat against my will the Worcester & Oxford. Here's another 2,500,000 of capital – I may say 8,000,000 and really all very likely to go on. And what is satisfactory all reflecting credit upon me and most of them forced upon me . . . Really my business is something extraordinary.*[64]

Now, Brunel decided, he had the means to make his move. In May 1836 he asked for Mary's hand in marriage and she accepted. In a letter to their aunt, Mary's sister, Fanny describes the proposal, which took place on a family walk along Holland Lane:

'He made her the offer as they were coming home, and told her he liked her all the five years he had known her, but would never engage her till he was fully able to keep a wife in comfort – I do admire his conduct very much, so honourable and forebearing – not shackling her with an endless engagement, as so many men would have done, but leaving her free, with her mind clear to enjoy pleasure, and to gain improvement and experience during the years of her youth . . . I always thought he admired and paid her more respect than anyone else, but never dreamed of it coming to this . . . I often said and thought that Mary would have chosen him before anyone else in the world.'[65]

Clearly, after the indecision expressed in his diaries back in

1828, Brunel had now decided that marriage was, after all, a good thing. His choice of Mary as his wife suggests (as his early diaries had) that he thought of marriage as something rather functional and of social usefulness, since Mary was – from the outside at least – something of a trophy wife. She was beautiful, and came from a good family, but she seems to have been the least interesting of the Horsley girls – displaying great poise rather than spontaneity or warmth. In their family plays, Mary would always take the more elegant roles, and she loved to dress up in extravagant gowns. In fact, her studied behaviour led her to be dubbed 'the Duchess of Kensington' by her sisters.

Mary offered fulfilment of a certain role, that of a truly lady-like wife. As the eldest sister, she had been responsible for looking after much of the running of the Horsley household and this – along with her striking appearance – was an attractive prospect for Brunel.

Finding a date for the wedding was difficult. By this stage, the summer of 1836, Brunel was incredibly busy with his work on the GWR, and it was hard for him to say where he would be on any particular day more than a week or so in advance. Everything was in place for married life, but the date. He had bought a new house, 18 Duke Street, an excellent London address backing on to St James's Park, which had plenty of room for a wife and family (and, of course, space for a large office on the ground floor, so that Brunel would never be far from his work).

Finally they settled on the date of 5 July, and Brunel and Mary were married in Kensington Church. Their honeymoon was brief, and can't have been the most entertaining time for Mary, since after just a few days in Capel Curig and along the Welsh border, they arrived in the West Country, where Brunel met Charles Saunders at Cheltenham to receive the latest news from the railway.

It was the shape of their marriage to come. Brunel's work remained dominant, while Mary, somewhat separately, played her part as the beautiful wife perfectly. She ran 18 Duke Street with efficiency, largely on her own. Brunel was often away on business and, after a trip to Italy on which she said the mountains made her dizzy, Mary chose to stay at home.[66] She was there to accompany Brunel whenever he needed her (to concerts or to ceremonies, such as the opening of a railway) and on these occasions she always looked elegant and refined. It was as if she were another badge of his achievement, which Brunel could display when required.

Accordingly, over the years, Mary's dress became more and more extravagant – she lavished money not just on dresses and jewellery but on decadently liveried coaches: 'she had, for morning use only, a carriage lined with green moiré silk while for evening she had another lined with the same in cream colour' and 'she never strolled in the park below her windows without a footman in livery following behind'.[67] Their house at Duke Street too became increasingly embellished and encrusted with ornaments, paintings, silver and china.

It is hard to know exactly what Brunel felt for Mary – he had given up the introspective style of writing that he used in his earlier Personal Diary. Despite all this, there was never any complaint (or at least no record of it) from either Mary or Brunel about their marriage.[68]

Interestingly, Brunel's marriage was in great contrast to that made by his father, Marc. After their dramatic meeting during the French Revolution, Marc and Sophia Brunel continued to have an intense love that lasted through their lifetimes. They could not bear to be apart; at the age of 76 Marc wrote to his wife: 'To you my *dearest* Sophia I am indebted for all my successes'. It is hard to imagine Brunel penning a similar line to Mary. Very few letters remain from their marriage; save for one that Brunel wrote from a hotel in Wootton Bassett, which is affectionate but over-ridingly pragmatic:

*My Dearest Mary,*

*. . . I am . . . going to sleep here – if I had been half an hour earlier I think I could not have withstood the temptation of coming up by the six? train, and returning by the morning goods train, just to see you; however, I will write you a long letter instead . . . here I am at the 'Cow and Candlesnuffers' or some such sign – a large room or cave, for it seems open to the wind everywhere . . . What's the use of the doors I can't conceive, for you might crawl under them if they happened to be locked, and they seem too crooked to open, the two ones with not a bad looking bit of glass between, seem particularly friendlily disposed . . .* [69]

Brunel's marriage remains something of an enigma. It may be that there is no more to know – that it seems rather formal because it was. Perhaps Brunel chose work as a wife after all, and Mary merely as an adornment.

Brunel returned from his honeymoon to a mark a celebration of his skills as an engineer. There was now sufficient money to start work on the Clifton Suspension Bridge again, and on 27 August 1836, Brunel and his new wife went to Bristol to attend the laying of the foundation stone. Hoards of cheering crowds came out to mark the occasion. The Marquis of Northampton, President of the British Association, led a procession, replete with bands, and buried under the stone several current coins, a chain plate bearing a picture of the bridge, a copy of the Act of Parliament and a plaque inscribed with the details of the bridge, including the name of the engineer.[70] Brunel revelled in the attention.

Isambard Kingdom Brunel had achieved what he had once thought impossible: he had a wife *and* a successful career as an engineer. But for him, it was still not enough.

# Global Vision of Transport: the *Great Western*

Brunel determined that his railway – the Great Western Railway – would be unlike any other in existence. The GWR was not the first railway in Britain but Brunel's unique vision made it the most revolutionary. This was not just a matter of the physical design, or its wider gauge. Existing railways carried goods such as coal from city to city at a moderate speed – along with a few passengers. They had grown piecemeal with no plan beyond linking up two places that required goods to be transported between them. Brunel had entirely new ideas. He saw that passengers rather than coal were the most important (and profitable) cargo, and that an integrated service would need to be planned.

His vision didn't stop with the railways. At a meeting of the directors in early 1835 there were concerns and misgivings expressed over the undertaking to build the 118-mile line. Brunel flippantly replied: 'Why not make it longer, and have a steamboat to go from Bristol to New York and call it the *Great Western?*' Most of the directors laughed at this joke, but Brunel and Guppy stayed up that night discussing the fantastic idea of a connected transport system, which would allow a passenger to step onto a train in London, and disembark in New York, having travelled the entire journey via a single service.

In October 1835, the GWR board of directors approved the plan. It was an incredibly radical idea, and would require an extraordinary ship. Not only was passenger rail travel new, but steamships were too – and certainly one had never been built that was capable of crossing the Atlantic. But that didn't deter Brunel.

Having only just started work on the GWR, the inexhaustibly ambitious Brunel would now turn his hand to the task of steamship design as well. He had no training whatsoever in marine engineering, but that didn't trouble him. Straight away, he and Guppy created 'The Great Western Steamship Company'.

While the project may have started as a quip, the new Steamship Company realised that this was a commercial hot potato, and from the outset tried to keep the project quiet to prevent others copying it. There was no advertising at first, and only six copies of the prospectus were issued, all hand-written. Business would be done by word-of-mouth.

As for Brunel, he now had two enormous and innovative projects to engineer at once. But while he dreamt up fantastic plans for transatlantic crossings, there were immediate and practical problems to be faced on the GWR.

The greatest obstacle on the London-Bristol line was the dramatically undulating landscape, that no steam train could climb. Brunel's survey had found the flattest possible route, but in order to also keep the line as straight and fast as possible the line had to go through hills and valleys, not around them. That meant the expensive construction of numerous ambitious bridges, viaducts and tunnels to maintain a level path. (In the end, Brunel achieved gradients so flat that the GWR was known as 'Brunel's Billiards Table'.)[71]

As they began to construct the two initial sections of the line – London to Maidenhead, and Bristol to Bath – it was clear from the outset that progress would be slower at the Bristol end where the Box Tunnel (the biggest engineering project on the line) had to be dug.

Work on the difficult Box Tunnel had to begin at once. Much of the almost two-mile-long tunnel[72] would have to be dug through a thick bed of greater oolitic limestone (later mined as Bath stone) and Brunel decided that although he would brick the west end of the tunnel, it should be safe to leave the east section, through the stone, unlined. It wasn't only Dionysus Lardner who said that this was an impossible structure; now the geologists launched a separate attack on Brunel, saying that, without a lining, it would collapse.

The west front of the Box Tunnel

Brunel carried on regardless. He hired the contractors Paxton & Orton, and they began by sinking six permanent shafts and two temporary ones into the hill, down to the level where the tunnel would run. Over 1,000 navvies were brought in, along with 100 horses to drag away the spoil. It was extremely hard work – digging through dense blue clay and limestone – and winter brought yet more difficulties when the shafts flooded. Paxton & Orton had to spend large amounts of money on steam pumps to drain the shafts. This put them under terrible financial strain, so Brunel went to the GWR directors for help. But the directors refused, the shafts re-filled with water, and the price of GWR shares fell. Doubts about Brunel began to creep in to the boardroom.

Nevertheless, work on the Box Tunnel resumed – this time the contractors were Brewer of Box and Lewis of Bath who were both used to digging the local stone. The shafts were completed, and work on the tunnel progressed slowly through the dense rock – one ton of gunpowder and one ton of candles were used each week for four and a half years. The navvies worked for up to 16 hours a day, moving weights of up to four-hundredweight regardless of the weather. They risked their lives daily, breathing in the sulphurous fumes of the explosives and at constant risk of flooding and quicksand. (Consequently, they were often drunk – in 1850 it was calculated that for every mile of railway built in Great Britain, £100 was spent on alcohol.[73]) But despite the many difficulties of digging the tunnel, there was never any sign of it collapsing (and still isn't to this day).

There is a legend that the tunnel is so aligned that on Brunel's birthday, 9 April, light shines directly through it, from end to end – as a memorial to its creator. If Brunel had wanted to do this, it would have been perfectly possible – there were reams of data available to him, listing the position of the sun on specific dates. But Brunel did not indulge himself on this occasion. After all, to make this happen, Brunel would have had to put a kink in the path of the tunnel – something he would never have done.

While the Box Tunnel took years to build, the London end of the line progressed much more quickly – the ground was flatter and there were fewer engineering works. The only major obstacle on the section to Maidenhead was the River Brent, and to cross this Brunel built the Wharncliffe Viaduct – a brick structure with nine arches, in Brunel's favoured Nubian Egyptian style.

But even here, at the London end, the work was slow. In addition to the implementation of an entirely new gauge, Brunel decided to redesign the track itself. The existing Liverpool and

# The Mirror

OF

## LITERATURE, AMUSEMENT, AND INSTRUCTION.

No. 923.]      SATURDAY, DECEMBER 1, 1838.      [Price 2d

## THE WHARNCLIFFE VIADUCT

### OF THE GREAT WESTERN RAILROAD, HANWELL, MIDDLESEX.

It is our intention to give an accurate architectural description of the Great Western Railway; to be illustrated by engravings. The engravings will appear occasionally before we publish the description, in order that they may be the more readily referred to, as they would be too numerous to be inserted with the description.

The Wharncliffe Viaduct connects two vast embankments, and runs parallel with the Uxbridge road, near the village of Hanwell, Middlesex; it consists of eight noble eliptical arches, springing from massive piers of brick, upon a stone base. The capitals of the piers, and the divisions and coping of the wall on each side of the road, are of stone. The armorial bearings of Lord Wharncliffe, boldly carved in stone, are placed over the centre pier of the viaduct; the Directors having paid this compliment to his Lordship, in acknowledgment of his exertions during the passing of the Act of Parliament for the erection of the railroad. The best view of the viaduct is from the Uxbridge road; the ground seen through the arches is a gentle eminence, upon which several villas are placed; the whole is thickly studded with trees, forming a parklike scene, of which the viaduct is the architectural ornament. The view from the top of the viaduct is extensive and beautiful; and it is from this spot that a birds eye view may be attained of that immense pile of building, the Hanwell Lunatic Asylum.

The pleasant little village of Hanwell is situated eight miles (W.) from London. The river Brent runs through the parish, and the Grand Junction Canal bounds it on the west. The celebrated classical scholar, Dr. H. Glasse, who distinguished himself by his Greek translation of Milton's Sampson Agonistes, was rector of Hanwell. James Hanway, a noted traveller and philanthropist, who died in 1786, was buried at Hanwell.

Brunel was responsible for the construction of the Great Western Railway's Wharncliffe Viaduct

Manchester Railways used stone blocks fitted with iron chairs to support the rails. Finding that this produced a rather bumpy ride, Brunel proposed to support the rails along their length with longitudinal timbers. These timbers were supported by ballast, and cross sleepers (or 'transoms') were fixed at 15-foot intervals.[74] He re-invented the rail, creating an inverted 'U' shape profile, which was much lighter (and therefore cheaper) than the original – an invention he refused to patent. The extra work in laying the track caused delays – as did waiting for deliveries of the novel rail and timbers (which had to be specially preserved or 'kyanized' before creosote became available in 1840).

It was clear that the opening date for the line, 1837, would not be met. And as the track from London-Maidenhead progressed, and Brunel turned his attention to the locomotives that would run on it, further problems arose. Supremely confident in his own abilities and reluctant as ever to delegate, Brunel began by designing the locomotives himself. He ordered two engines, making stipulations for the engine-builders to follow which were not only inefficient, but would counteract any of the benefits of speed and smoothness that he had hoped to achieve with the broad gauge. He insisted that the 'standard velocity' should be considered 30mph and the piston speed should not exceed 280 feet per minute. To achieve this would require huge wheels with a diameter of 7–10 feet (whereas the biggest wheels to date were 5 ft 6in in diameter). But Brunel's second stipulation – that the engine weight should not exceed 10.5 tons if mounted on six wheels, or 8 tons if mounted on four – meant that the locomotives couldn't carry big enough boilers to drive these great wheels. In short, the designs were disastrous. For all Brunel's talents, he could not list locomotive engineer among them.

In July 1837, Brunel received a letter that would prove to be his salvation (although he would never say as much). It was from a young man named Daniel Gooch, presenting himself as available for work. Not only did he have experience working for Robert Stephenson in Newcastle but, having worked on two locomotives of 5ft 6in gauge for the New Orleans Railway, he was also a fan of the wider gauge. On 9 August Gooch met Brunel for the first time and on Monday 14 August (ten days before Gooch turned 21) he started work at the GWR's depot at West Drayton.

The first engines (those ordered by Brunel) arrived in November 1837: Mather Dixon's *Premier* and Charles Tayleur's *Vulcan*. Gooch's heart must have sunk into his workboots when he saw them. But he had a solution. One of the locomotives he had designed for New Orleans – *North Star* – hadn't been shipped due to financial reasons. So Gooch bought *North Star* to add to Brunel's locomotives, and it was by far the best in an otherwise ramshackle fleet.

Gooch's early days at the GWR were a great test of his character and loyalty to Brunel. Having acquired *North Star,* he soon added *Morning Star* to their fleet – but the rest of their locomotives (chosen by Brunel) were hopeless, and it was left to Gooch to take the flack from the GWR board of directors. He did so without implicating Brunel.

This loyalty – and the fact that Gooch stood up to Brunel – would eventually earn him Brunel's respect and friendship, despite the fact that the two men were very different in character. While Brunel was chasing his 'castles in the air', revelling in invention and searching for fame, Gooch led an austere, rather puritanical life and for him work was simply a duty and a means to money.

Gooch's arrival at the GWR was a great help to Brunel, who was under great pressure. He was not only engineer to the GWR railway (where he concerned himself with every detail of track, locomotive and every bridge and tunnel), but in 1836 had also taken the position of Engineer to the Oxford, Worcester & Wolverhampton railway and also to the South Devon Railway from Exeter to Plymouth. There was also the not insignificant matter of an enormous steamship.

Work had begun swiftly on the ship, the *Great Western*. In fact, the project seemed to benefit from having less of Brunel's attention than he gave to the railway: he had created a building committee of himself and three of his trusted allies: Captain Christopher Claxton (the ex-navy officer); Thomas Guppy; and William Patterson, in whose Bristol shipyard the *Great Western* would be built. This left Brunel in a position that allowed him to do what he did best: conjure up ideas and pursue them, marketing them with flair and relentless energy. In contrast to his simultaneous work on the GWR, in this case Brunel co-operated rather than controlled, and the results were much improved.

With the *Great Western* – as with the GWR – Brunel was fighting convention, circumstances in which he was in his element. At the time, steamships were becoming more popular, but were still small and designed chiefly to steam in shallow waters around the coast, or – more adventurously – across the Irish Sea to Dublin. The universally held belief was that no steamship could carry enough fuel to cross the Atlantic.[75] Once again, Dionysius Lardner sprang to Brunel's opposition, and announced at the 1835 meetings of the British Association for the Advancement of Science in Dublin and Liverpool, that people 'might as well talk of making a trip from Liverpool or New York to the moon'.[76] Lardner argued that it would be impossible to build a steamship capable of crossing the Atlantic because the increased amount of coal needed would require a bigger hull, which in turn would need more coal to drive it . . . and so on, in an vicious circle. And that was before cargo was added.

Brunel realised that this was not the case. While the volume of a hull increases in cubic yards, its surface – which is the area in contact with the water – increases only in square yards. This meant that the coal-carrying capacity of the hull could be increased without resulting in a prohibitive increase in water resistance. In fact, as the size of a ship is increased, the volume devoted to fuel could be decreased. What's more, the longer ship would be smoother and faster in the water. Brunel wasn't the first to realise this 'cubic law' (as he admitted[77]), but he was the first to fully exploit it.

To research how steamships were built, Claxton, Guppy and Patterson visited shipyards in Glasgow and Liverpool and reported back; Brunel then drew up the designs. The result was (at the time) the longest ship in the world: a timber-hulled paddle steamer of huge dimensions: 236 feet long, with a displacement of 2,300 tons. The engines alone were enormous, and Brunel would only entrust their building to the best – not the cheapest – company (a principle he had stated to the Clifton Bridge committee); Maudsley Son & Field, who had already built several marine engines.

Brunel had a role in the design of the engine however, introducing a variable cut-off device, which reduced the amount of steam entering the cylinder on each piston stroke, thereby economising on the use of the expensive vapour.[78] He realised that just a small amount of steam introduced into the cylinder would continue to heat up and expand under the compression of the piston. Again, although Brunel could have patented this change, he chose not to. This was a principle he abided to throughout his career – despite the great loss of potential earnings – believing that patents stifled healthy competition and progress. In later years this would also cost him a good deal of glory. For instance, in 1852 Brunel designed a polygonally-bored rifle, which would put on a spin on the bullet so that it fired more accurately. He made at least one test model, but allowed Joseph Whitworth to take the patent and full credit for the invention.

Brunel also made changes to the body of the ship, making it strong enough to resist any storm: to the great oak hull he added an unusually large number of iron trusses, and he secured the keel ribs with iron bolts to provide extra strength. The bottom of the boat was covered in copper, to resist the shipworm

*Teredo navalis*, which although it had the distinction of having inspired his father's Tunnel Shield, was still a frequent destroyer of ships.

As the *Great Western* neared completion, it became clear that the plan to use her to cross the Atlantic had got out, and her progress was being closely watched. A rival company, the British & American Steam Navigation Company of Liverpool, had also set its sights on taking the glory (and the profits) of being the first

The steamship *Great Western* passing Portishead on her first voyage to New York

steamship to cross the Atlantic, and had begun construction of *British Queen* for exactly this purpose. But on seeing how quickly the *Great Western* was progressing, they temporarily shelved *British Queen* and brought in a much smaller ship, the 703-ton *Sirius*, originally intended only for Anglo-Irish crossings.

On Wednesday 28 March 1838, the *Sirius* departed for New York, carrying a crew of 35, and 40 passengers. Meanwhile, the *Great Western* was still undergoing trials at Bristol. The *Sirius* already had a head-start of three days when, on 31 March, the *Great Western* finally left Bristol with Guppy, Claxton and Brunel on board to witness the maiden voyage.

After two hours of travelling, there was a distinct smell of oil and burning on board the *Great Western*, and smoke and flames curled up from around the base of the funnel. The engine room was on fire. Claxton armed himself with a hand-operated fire-pump and rushed down into the thick smoke of the engine room. As he struggled with the pump, he was struck on the head and knocked to the ground by a heavy object from above. He righted himself, and saw that he had been hit by the body of a man, who was now lying unconscious and facedown in the water accumulating from the fire-pumps. In the thick smoke Claxton couldn't see who it was. He picked up the body, and had it hoisted to safety. Only on deck did Claxton realise whose life he had saved: his friend Brunel.

Brunel had been climbing down a ladder which – charred by the fire – had snapped under his weight, so that he fell 20 feet – and onto Claxton.

Once the fire was out, Brunel was lowered off the ship at Canvey Island: his injuries were serious and he had to stay there several weeks. It was 8 April before the *Great Western* departed again for New York, this time without Brunel – although he continued to issue instructions from his sickbed. There were only seven passengers on board – the other 50 had cancelled where they heard sensationalised reports of the fire.

The *Sirius* now had a substantial lead, but after almost two weeks at sea her crew were running very low on fuel and were forced to burn some of the cargo to keep her going; this was just as Lardner and others had predicted for a conventional steamship.

But the unconventional *Great Western* had no such problems, and sped on, closing the gap as much as possible.

On 22 April, the *Sirius* docked at New York, after a journey of 19 days from Cork. The same day, the *Great Western* docked off Sandy Hook – arriving later than the *Sirius;* she had just missed being the first steamship across the Atlantic, but she had done the journey much faster, in the time of 15 days and five hours, and having travelled the extra 220 miles from Bristol. On arrival, there were 200 tons of coal remaining on the *Great Western,* but only 15 on the *Sirius.*

Brunel had proved his point: the *Great Western* – able to carry large quantities of cargo, passengers and fuel with ease – was in a different league to the *Sirius*, and she ushered in a new era of transport. She went on to make 67 crossings in eight years.

The *Great Western* was the result of Brunel's brilliant and insightful design – and his unshakeable belief in his own calculations. But she was also the product of a great collaborative effort, between Brunel, Guppy, Claxton and Patterson. Unfortunately, this was in sharp contrast to Brunel's work on the Great Western Railway, where he pursued his own beliefs almost exclusively, to the cost of the project. Exactly at the time when the *Great Western* proved such a success, Brunel was getting into deeper and deeper trouble with his railway.

# Brunel Under Pressure

As the deadline for the opening of the first section of the GWR line from London to Maidenhead approached, Brunel's workload became unbearably large. The huge task began to take its toll on Brunel. Usually a man of indefatigable strength and bravura, under the pressure of a massive project that he had taken almost entirely on his shoulders alone, and the increasingly critical Board of Directors, his resilience began to flag. He was entering a period in which, for the first time, failure was a real possibility. On 3 December 1837, Brunel wrote with uncharacteristic vulnerability to his good friend on the GWR Board of Directors, Charles Saunders:

*If ever I go mad, I shall have the ghost of the opening of the railway walking before me, or rather standing in front of me, holding out its hand, and when it steps forward, a little swarm of devils in the shape of leaky pickle-tanks, uncut timber, half-finished station houses, sinking embankments, broken screws, absent guard plates, unfinished drawings and sketches, will, quietly and quite as a matter of course and as if I ought to have expected it, lift up my ghost and put him a little further off than before.*[79]

Brunel was already behind schedule with the railway. The Directors had announced in August 1837 that the first section of the line would open in November. Brunel had missed that deadline, and a number of obstacles meant that, realistically, the line would not open for several more months.

Pressure was piling up on Brunel from all sides. On 18 May 1837, Mary had given birth to their first child, Isambard. Usually an occasion of pure joy, this event was initially marred by the fact that the child was born with a deformity, one leg being considerably shorted than the other. The deformity was not bad, but Mary – always concerned about appearances – was shocked and worried by it, but would not allow her son to be operated upon. This can only have added to Isambard's stress at this difficult time. (The deformity didn't hold Isambard junior back. He went on to become a successful lawyer, and Chancellor of the Diocese of Ely.)

By April the next year, the first section of line was still not open, and there remained a long list of problems facing Brunel: despite ongoing efforts the Hanwell embankment remained waterlogged and sinking; almost 20 miles of track had yet to be laid; and the locomotives still had to be test-run.

On 11 May he wrote to Thomas Guppy: *I am nervous, anxious and unhappy – in fact, blue devilish. An infinite number of thoughts crowding in upon me, requiring attention and thought – all in arrears and I am quite incapable of getting through them. Everything seeming to go wrong – we talk of the 30th for opening and now everyone believes it – but me. I suppose I need a dose of salts.*[80]

A great surge of effort by the navvies fortunately proved Brunel wrong. On 31 May, a private opening of the line from London to Maidenhead was held for the GWR Directors and their friends – 300 in all. Marc and Sophia were there, and Mary (elegantly) accompanied Brunel. The *North Star* made the first journey from Paddington to Maidenhead in 49 minutes – an average speed of 28mph. This increased to $33^1/_3$ on the return journey. Spirits were high, especially those of Thomas Guppy, who ran along the tops of the carriages as they sped along.

But when the track opened to the public on 4 June, it only brought more problems for Brunel. The ill-conceived locomotives were unreliable and feeble, incapable of reaching any good speed no matter what the state of the track. After Brunel's great promises, the re-designed track was a disappointment, producing an extremely bumpy and uncomfortable ride – and it cost over £500 more per mile than the old stone method.[81]

With use the line got even worse. After just a month, the weight of the trains had distorted the track, making it even bumpier; Brunel had used sand and fine ballast under the rails and he now had to acknowledge this was a mistake.

All this aroused a growing discontent within the Board of Directors. Although Brunel had his friends on the board – such as Gibbs and Saunders – there were now too many shareholders for Brunel to rely on friendship alone for support. In fact, by July 1838, one group of shareholders were intent on removing Brunel from the project altogether. These Northern businessmen (who became known as the 'Liverpool Group') believed that the only way to build a railway was Stephenson's way, and they opposed almost everything Brunel did.

The directors began to wonder whether, despite all Brunel's modifications, the track might even be worse than the original, Stephensonian narrow gauge. So a party of four of them – including George Henry Gibbs and Charles Saunders – tried out the line from Euston to Denbigh Hall. They found it rough and bumpy – no better than Brunel's. But since Brunel had promised that the broad gauge would be a great improvement on the narrow gauge, he still wasn't off the hook.

Brunel was aware of the attacks on his work and suggested that two independent engineers be called in to assess the line, and report back to the Board. The Board approached James Walker (President of the Institute of Civil Engineers) and Robert Stephenson but they both refused – although Stephenson was Brunel's rival in designing the railways, the two men had a mutual respect that would develop into a lifelong friendship.

In August 1838, things came to a head. At the half-yearly meeting in Bristol on 15 August, the Liverpool Group directly confronted Brunel for the first time. They pressed for an Engineer to work alongside Brunel, plus their representation on the board. They could easily have won and quashed both Brunel and the Broad Gauge on that day, since they had a majority – but for the fact that they didn't know it. George Gibbs, who knew the numbers, kept them to himself to safeguard his friend Brunel.

But the Liverpool Group continued their complaints, and so at the end of August the GWR Board once more took up Brunel's idea of inviting two independent engineers to assess the GWR line. This time they secured John Hawkshaw (then Engineer to the Manchester & Leeds Railway and a follower of Stephenson, chosen by the Liverpool Group) and Nicholas Wood, who brought with him the irrepressible Dionysius Lardner.

Only Hawkshaw's report was ready for the next meeting, on 10 October. Brunel was there to defend himself. Hawkshaw was Brunel's junior, and this must have been an excruciating process for Brunel, who was as proud as he was talented.

Hawkshaw's report was highly critical of Brunel's line, but also vague and badly researched; at one point, he stated that the GWR's locomotives were over-powered, which they certainly were not. It made little mention of the main concern, the permanent way (and in fact Gibbs observed 'the greater part of [the report] might have been written without coming near the line'[82]). But Hawkshaw did point out that by deviating from the standard (narrow) gauge, the GWR was at risk of isolating itself. Brunel countered that the GWR was extending into areas where no other railways had reached – and once the GWR was completed no other lines would be needed.

The second report, from Wood and Lardner, was received on 12 December. Wood was also critical of the broad gauge and its high cost. His clearest criticism was that Brunel had introduced too many piles into the track, which (as well as being costly) created a rough ride. In addition, he had included comparisons of broad and narrow gauge locomotives, detailed in an appendix by Lardner. Experiments with *North Star* suggested a very poor performance at speed which was due, Lardner said, to the great wind resistance of the large surface area of the front of the locomotive.

The over-ridingly negative tone of the report was enough to convince even Brunel's allies, Gibbs and Saunders, that another engineer should be engaged on the project. A number of the directors, including Gibbs, Saunders, Casson and Russell, went to see Brunel at his home, 18 Duke Street, to tell him of their decision to appoint a second Engineer. Brunel's response was decisive, and took the directors by surprise; they could have his resignation, but he would not share his position as Engineer of the Great Western Railway. The threat of his resignation was not empty, as the diary of George Henry Gibbs reveals:

'Brunel . . . in a very modest way said that the evidence which was accumulating against him appeared to be too great to be resisted without injury to the Company, and therefore he was prepared to give way. He had no vanity of any kind. If it were necessary to yield, he had no objection to it being said that he had been defeated, for he felt confident in the correctness of his views and was sure that he should have opportunities of proving it'.[83]

Brunel had reached a crisis point; the pressure was piling onto him from all sides – problems were reported with all aspects of the railway: the track, the locomotives and the engineering works (including the Box Tunnel). He was on the point of giving in. But as Gibbs' diary shows, at his lowest ebb Brunel drew on the strength of his conviction that he was right. Having been knocked down, he now set out to show his worth – and to prove Lardner wrong, once more.

Brunel and Gooch began a series of experiments on the *North Star*, in the hope of modifying the engine to make her faster, in spite of what Lardner said about her wind resistance. They immediately saw that the blast pipe was too small, which was causing pressure to build in the cylinders, and also that it was placed in such a way that it was only exerting a small effect on the fire.

The Rocket and the North Star

By moving the blast pipe and increasing its size, Brunel and Gooch drastically improved the performance of the engine. Brunel was depressed and exhausted, but they worked furiously, even on Christmas Day, to bring the engine up to scratch.

On 29 December, they gave George Gibbs and some of the other directors a sneak preview of their achievements; the *North Star* pulled them on a train weighing 43 tons from Paddington to Maidenhead. Gibbs reports that: 'We carried 43 tons of carriages and load at an average rate of 38 miles an hour, consuming only 0.95 lbs of coke per ton of net weight per mile'[84] – much faster than Lardner's calculations would allow.

The shareholders next meeting was on 9 January 1839 Brunel's opponents, the Liverpool Group readied themselves to dispatch Brunel and his broad gauge railway. They moved that Brunel's plans 'are injudicious, expensive, and ineffectual for their professed objects and therefore ought not to be proceeded with'.[85] But then Brunel played his trump card: he revealed the new and improved performance of the *North Star*, which clearly refuted the objections of Lardner and his colleagues. A vote was taken – the Liverpool party was defeated by 1,645 votes.[86] Brunel and the broad gauge would remain.

It was a great personal victory for Brunel, but ultimately a shot in the foot for the GWR. The narrow gauge was already so well established that there was little chance of converting it to broad gauge. And having two sizes of gauge in one country was impracticable: passengers would have to dismount and change trains every time the two gauges met. Nevertheless, Brunel believed that the other railways would see the wisdom in his design and adopt it, and so he continued obstinately with his plan, now with the indisputable backing of the GWR's shareholders.

Brunel had won this battle to keep the broad gauge, but his trial was not over yet. Gooch had been asked to submit a report on the Company's locomotives at the same shareholder's meeting, and although he tried to protect Brunel, it was impossible for Gooch to present the facts without implicating him in the design of the first ill-conceived locomotives. Brunel chose to interpret this as disloyalty; but was more enraged that the result was that Gooch was asked to report directly to the board. This effectively put Gooch on a par with Brunel – a situation that did not please Brunel at all.

Nevertheless, Brunel had survived the attack from the Liverpool Group and it was hoped that work might proceed more quickly now that their criticisms had been silenced.

The next section of the west end of the line had to cross the River Thames at Maidenhead, where the river was 100 yards wide. It was Brunel's priority here– as ever – to maintain a flat gradient, and yet (as the Thames Commission insisted) he had to allow for sailing barges, with their tall masts, to pass underneath. The Commission also insisted that neither the towpath nor the channel should be obstructed, leaving opportunity for just one bridge pier in the middle of the river.

Brunel's solution was elegant: a low bridge with the flattest arches ever built. Immediately, the design was attacked: his critics were convinced it would collapse. Brunel had faith in his own calculations, but in the summer of 1838, towards the end of the bridge's construction, the bricks in the eastern arch began to sag and its shape started to distort, much to the delight of his critics. It turned out that the contractor, Mr Chadwick, had eased away the supports too early, before the cement had set. Mr Chadwick repaired his mistake, but Brunel asked him to leave the supports in place: although they were no longer holding the bridge they looked like they were. They remained for nine months – Brunel's private joke that his critics believed his bridge needed support when all along it was free-standing. When the supports were finally blown away by a storm, the bridge had been carrying trains for months.[87]

The Maidenhead Bridge was typical of Brunel's flair in designing the engineering works along the GWR. He paid attention to every detail – right down to the design of the lampposts. He intended to make every station an architectural delight, a temple of engineering – this desire to 'overbuild' beyond the minimum antagonised the Board of Directors who constantly tried to rein him in. At Reading Station, there was visible evidence of this clash of values. In 1839, Brunel had drawn up plans for Reading, and initially had them approved; but when the Committee saw the cost of the plans they withdrew their approval. Brunel went ahead and built a station – but to punish their parsimony he made it as unattractive as he could.

While Brunel pushed on with extending the line through Slough, Reading and Didcot, Gooch – with growing autonomy – began to expand the fleet of locomotives. He believed he could improve upon *North Star* and *Morning Star* and in 1839 began the design of a new class of locomotives. He took inspiration from Stephenson's *Stars*, but changed their dimensions and their engine power, increasing the size of their boiler.

First of this new class of locomotives was *Firefly*. On 14 March 1840 she was used to pull the Director's Special on a trip to Reading. On the way back she averaged 50 mph – a sustained speed that was unheard-of in 1840. In fact, despite his almost obsessive emphasis on achieving speed in the GWR, Brunel became concerned about speeding on his lines, and wrote to Gooch:

*J Hill brought up the Cyclops in 27 minutes from Slough following the short train into Paddington within three minutes. This work must be put to a stop effectually. The Directors have determined to fine him ten shillings.*[88]

But to inhibit daring was against Brunel's nature; his love of adventure broke through and he soon refunded the driver's ten shillings. By 1842, the locomotives on the GWR and Bristol &

Exeter railways – designed by Gooch, on a track created by Brunel –would be the fastest in the world. At last, Brunel's hard work was starting to pay off.

With a growing fleet of locomotives, it was clear that the GWR would need somewhere to store them as space was growing short at the makeshift Paddington Station. On 13 September 1840, Gooch wrote to Brunel suggesting that the 'best site for our principal engine establishment' was near Swindon, a small market town at the time. Brunel designed not only the depot buildings, but also 300 houses for the people who would come to work there (his interest in 'model' housing was somewhat ahead of his time) and the layout of 'New Swindon', including a church and other public buildings. The works would open on 2 January 1843, and it was there at Swindon that another enduring feature of railway travel was born: the unpalatable refreshment stop.

A hotel was built within Swindon station, and the GWR Company let it out on a long-term contract that (rather foolishly) included a stipulation that all regular trains should stop there 'for a reasonable period of about ten minutes' so that passengers could stretch their legs and get a drink. This luxurious monopoly was soon abused by the hotel owners, who watered down the drinks and used anything but the finest ingredients.

By the end of 1840, Brunel was vastly over budget and past his deadline. The original finish

Brunel was incensed by the state of the coffee at Swindon and wrote to the first proprietor of the hotel:

Dear Sir,

I assure you, Mr. Player was wrong in supposing that I thought you purchased inferior coffee. I thought I said to him that I was surprised you should buy such bad roasted corn. I did not believe you had such a things as coffee in the place; I am sure I never tasted any. I have long ceased to make complaints at Swindon. I avoid taking anything there when I can help it.

Yours faithfully,
I.K. Brunel

date had been set for August 1840, and in December of that year the work was still in progress. There were still major works underway at Sonning (where a huge cutting was dug) and near Cheltenham, and the most difficult link – the Box Tunnel – was still unfinished.

Brunel set a completion date of February 1841 and – after that came and went – he threw all the manpower he could find at this last obstacle. Four thousand men and 300 horses worked around the clock to finish the tunnel. By the end of June 1841, the tunnel was finally completed (one line of it at least) – at the cost of the lives of more than 100 navvies. On 3 June 1841, the first public train travelled from Paddington, London to Bristol in a time of five and a half hours – a journey that would have taken 15–20 hours by stagecoach. But the final cost of the London to Bristol line was £5,877,120, more than double Brunel's initial estimate of £2,085,330.[89]

By the time Brunel had finished the line, he had laid 118 miles of track. Along the way, he had been publicly scrutinised and on these occasions he had not only survived, but come out triumphant. In 1835, Brunel had written in his diary that the GWR would be 'the finest work in England'.[90] It had certainly established Brunel as a leading engineer; a well-known, if controversial, figure.

# Brunel Gets Famous: the *Great Britain*

On 3 April 1843 Brunel was demonstrating a talent beyond the usual repertoire of a civil engineer. He was performing magic. Brunel now had two sons: Isambard, and Henry Marc, and he was entertaining them at Duke Street with conjuring tricks. One of these involved hiding a half-sovereign in his mouth, but as he did this, he accidentally swallowed. The coin slipped from his mouth and lodged in his windpipe; it was stuck fast, and threatened to choke him. The coin was deep in his trachea – no amount of coughing could shift it – and was still there several weeks later.

Several eminent physicians considered the problem, but could not come up with a solution. So Brunel designed a pair of specially-made long-handled forceps, which were to be inserted through an incision into his windpipe. The surgeon Sir Benjamin Brodie performed the tricky operation (after which the forceps became known as 'Brodie's forceps'). But the forceps couldn't reach the coin and it stayed put.

Isambard and Mary had three children. After Isambard came Henry (born in 1842) and Florence (born around 1847; there is no clear record of the date). Henry became an engineer, including Tower Bridge amongst his projects. He did not marry. Although Isambard – who became an ecclesiastical lawyer – did marry, he had no children, so it was left to Florence to carry on the Brunel line. She married a master at Eton College, Arthur James, and it was through their daughter Celia (who married into the Noble family) that the Brunel family line continued.[91]

Brunel tried to shake the coin lose, but to no avail. His father Marc – who with Sophia was living at Duke Street at the time – came up with the next idea. He devised a table to which Brunel would be strapped and turned upside-down. On the second attempt with the table, on 13 May, the coin finally popped out of Isambard's mouth.

On hearing this news, an acquaintance of Brunel's, the historian and politician Thomas Macaulay, apparently rushed through the Athenaeum Club shouting 'It's out! It's out!' and everyone knew what he was talking about.[92] *The Times* – who had been following Brunel's progress – gave the liberation of the coin a full report on 16 May 1843. That Brunel's swallowing of a sovereign was a matter of national interest was indicative of his growing reputation. Having built the GWR line from London to Bristol, and constructed the world's first transatlantic steamship, Brunel was now becoming a household name.

And at this time, his fame was about to swell – he was about to launch a second steamship, even more revolutionary than the *Great Western*. The original idea of the Great Western Steam Company had been to build a sister ship to the *Great Western*, but Brunel, as always, had higher ambitions.

The inspiration for a radically different structure came one day in October 1838, when Brunel was standing in Bristol's Floating Harbour. A small paddle-steamer, the *Rainbow*, came in. Brunel was intrigued to see that the vessel was made not from wood but from iron; in fact, the first iron-hulled ship, the *Aaron Manby*, had gone to sea in 1821, but since Brunel was not a marine engineer, he wasn't aware of it.[93] He asked Captain Claxton and William Patterson to try out the ship by joining the *Rainbow* on her next trip, which was to Antwerp.

Claxton and Patterson were impressed by the iron hull, and so Brunel – along with the same committee who had built the *Great Western,* (Claxton, Patterson and Guppy) – made this the basis of the design for his new ship. True to form, Brunel's design was rather out of the ordinary. He planned to build the largest iron-hulled steamship to date: while the largest iron-hulled ships at the time weighed around 500 tons, Brunel's would weigh more than 3,000. Nothing like it had ever been built before.

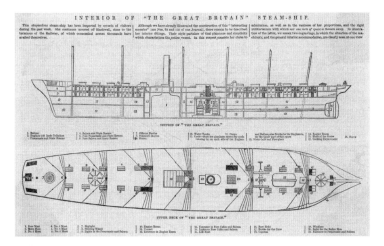

A plan of the SS *Great Britain*

Brunel submitted five designs for the ship to the Directors of the Great Western Steamship Company before his plan was accepted: a 3,444-ton paddle-steamer with an iron hull. At this size, the *Great Britain* was too large to get through the lock-gates of the Cumberland Basin in Bristol's Docks, and so, as Brunel commenced building works in a specially-constructed dry dock next to the Floating Harbour, he got the assurance of the Bristol Docks that they would widen the lock when the time for launch came.

Construction began on 18 July 1839 when the keel girders were laid down. But on this project – as with the GWR – there quickly developed some opposition between Brunel and the Steamship Company Directors. As with the *Great Western*, Brunel wanted his steam engines not to be built by the cheapest contractor but by the best – and again, he suggested the company Maudsley Son & Field. This time, the Directors over-ruled him and chose Francis Humphreys, the cheapest. Unfortunately, Humphreys was immediately out of his depth; his company (Messrs Hall of Dartford) didn't have machinery of sufficient size to build Brunel's mammoth engines. So, when the Great Western Steamship Company instructed them to build the machinery as well, he was saddled with an even more daunting job.

In May 1840, Brunel's eye was caught once more by a new technology, on a 200-ton ship entering the Bristol Docks. The SS *Archimedes* was a test-ship for the screw propeller (an invention patented by Francis Pettit Smith in 1836) and it immediately impressed Brunel.[94] This time, Guppy was sent to try out the novel vessel, as she steamed to Liverpool. He returned with a very favourable report.

Despite the fact that the *Great Britain*'s hull was already built up to the level of the paddle-boxes, and Humphreys was working on the paddle-engines, Brunel suspended work while he undertook the first scientific comparison of paddle-wheel and screw propulsion, using data from the *Great Western* and the *Archimedes*.

He submitted a full report to the Company Directors pointing out the advantages of the reduced weight and simpler hull form of the screw design. Brunel was emphatic – *my conviction of the wisdom, I may almost say the necessity of our adopting the improvement I now recommend is too strong, and I feel it is too well founded, for me to hesitate or shrink from the responsibility*[95] – and the Directors were convinced. This however meant that work would have to begin again from scratch, despite a lack of funds (the Company relied solely on income from the *Great Western* steamship, and this was not bringing the financial rewards they had hoped for – although in large part, this was the fault of the poor state of Bristol's Ports, which had silted up again – rather than any fault of the ship[96]).

The hull would have to be re-built, with flush sides (there was no need for paddle boxes now) and the engines which had been designed to drive the paddles would have to be replaced with a new design capable of driving a screw propeller.

For Humphreys, who was already struggling with the size of the engines, it was all too much. He was exhausted, and simply couldn't cope with the thought of starting all over again. He buckled under the strain and died a few days later.

Brunel began the design of the ship again – a 16-foot iron propeller would be driven by new engines, creating an unprecedented 1,600 bhp (for comparison, the *Great Western* engines each produced 450 bhp). He added a feed-water heater, which used the waste heat coming from the base of the funnels (the source of the fire on the *Great Western*) to heat the water passing into the engine. Most importantly, since Brunel was building the hull from a new material, he considered its design from first principles, eschewing the conventional rib design. Instead, he placed great emphasis on longitudinal strength: he ran ten iron girders along the bottom of the ship, (securing the iron deck to their tops), and five watertight bulkheads across its width (creating compartments for the engines and coal bunkers). The levels of the ship were created by two more longitudinal bulkheads. (This design presaged the cellular construction of watertight compartments that Brunel would introduce on his next ship, the *Great Eastern*.)

Brunel was now a man of some reputation, and as he embarked on constructing the *Great Britain* to this innovative design, people took notice. The Admiralty got wind of it, and Sir Edward Parry (Controller of Steam Machinery for the Navy Board) requested Brunel's help in testing the screw propeller for the use of the Royal Navy.[97] What followed was a frustrating – even farcical – episode for Brunel, whose intent on action was matched only by the Navy's stultifying bureaucracy.

The clash of cultures was obvious from the outset. Brunel had a longstanding dislike of officialdom and any government schemes that interfered with individual action and responsibility. Equally, many of those in the Navy were suspicious of, and threatened by, Brunel and his reforming ways. But Brunel realised that the tests might provide him with valuable information which he might use to move improve the *Great Britain*, so he co-operated.[98] He was asked by the Admiralty to supervise the testing of a screw-propelled vessel. Brunel, used to working under commercial time constraints, drew up the plans for the engines within a fortnight, and got Maudsley, Sons & Field to make them. But when Brunel questioned the Admiralty on the whereabouts of the hull they had no answer; work on it had not even begun. It was clear that certain members of the Admiralty were blocking Brunel's efforts.

Brunel was summoned to meet with Sir George Cockburn, the First Sea Lord, over the affair of the missing ship. He arrived to find Cockburn in a rage – but over a different matter. The model of a sail-powered warship which sat on his desk had been vandalised: a section of the stern had been chopped off to make way for a roughly-attached screw propeller, and a label had been added: 'Mr Brunel's Mode of Applying the Screw to Her Majesty's Ships'.

Brunel managed to pacify Cockburn, and explained that this was most definitely not his doing. Finally, Cockburn was convinced, and as he went to instruct his subordinates to find the real culprits, Brunel quietly pulled out his pen-knife and scratched off the offending label.

The Navy next offered Brunel the *Acheron* to be fitted with the screw propeller and engine. When Brunel pointed out to them that the vessel was completely unsuitable, the response was months of silence. Frustrated, he sent in his resignation, and this finally spurred them into action. But it was not the action Brunel wanted – this time, the Navy offered him the *Rattler* – not much of an improvement on the *Acheron*. Brunel fitted the *Rattler* with engines and a screw propeller, but distanced himself from the trials that she was then used for.

In one test, the *Rattler* was tied to a steam paddler, the *Alecto*, and both boats then tried to pull against the other, in a river-bound tug of war. The *Rattler* won, pulling the *Alecto* away at a rate of 2.8 knots. The screw propeller proved its worth, and from 1845 the Royal Navy's ships were fitted with the screw rather than paddle wheels. But Brunel was so unimpressed by the bureaucracy of the Admiralty that he didn't even ask for payment – nor did he receive credit for his work.

Meanwhile, the construction of the *Great Britain* had been completed, and on 19 July 1843 she was launched with great ceremony. Prince Albert travelled on a special GWR train from Paddington – driven by Gooch and with Brunel standing beside him on the footplate. On the train with them was Francis Pettit Smith, inventor of the screw propeller.

At the Bristol terminus, Temple Meads station, there were excited crowds to greet them. Six hundred people sat down to a great banquet in the patternmakers' shop, before the Prince Consort gallantly stepped aside to allow Mrs Miles, one of the director's wives to name the ship.[99] When Mrs Miles' bottle missed, Albert stepped in anyway. The *Great Britain* then glided out into the Floating Harbour where she would be fitted with her engines and boilers.

By March 1844, she was ready to go. But the Bristol Docks Company had not honoured their agreement with Brunel that the docks would be widened to allow the enormous ship through. The delay was blamed on the fact that an Act of Parliament was required to make the changes. It took a whole year for this to be done, and it was January 1845 before the *Great Britain* left Bristol. Even then, she was not ready for her maiden voyage; there was yet more fitting-out to be done at Blackwall, in London.

There, she was visited by Queen Victoria and Prince Albert who inspected the 64 staterooms on board and admired the 1,200 yards of specially woven Brussels carpet[100] – and since the Queen could not go 'below stairs' to see the engines, Brunel demonstrated how they worked using a model he had made specially.

Crowds gathered in Bristol to watch the launch of the SS *Great Britain*, 19 July 1843

Finally, on 26 July 1845, the longest ship in the world set sail from Liverpool for New York. Although her capacity was vast – she could carry 252 first- and second-class passengers and 130 crew – the ship was disappointingly empty, with only 45 passengers and 600 tons of cargo on board. Technically, however, the *Great Britain* was a triumph and she made the crossing in just 14 days and 21 hours.

But just over one year later, in the autumn of 1846, the fortunes of the *Great Britain* took a turn for the worse. On 22 September, she left Liverpool for New York, carrying 180 passengers – the largest number to date on a transatlantic steamer. As they steamed out, dark fell and driving rain set in. Within only a few hours of travelling, the Master of the ship, Captain Hosken, was lost. A new lighthouse had been switched on just a few months earlier and this only added to Hosken's confusion. Mistaking the light for that of the Calf of Man at the southwest tip of the Isle of Man; Hosken changed course.[101] As the iron hull hit the rocks there was a huge grating screech of metal on stone. The ship had run aground. The passengers screamed in terror; the night was passed in confusion.

The promenade deck of the SS *Great Britain*, the first iron-hulled screw propeller-dr

As dawn broke, their real location became apparent. Hoskins saw the mountains of Mourne, and realised the ship was not stuck at the Isle of Man at all, but in Dundrum Bay, Northern Ireland. The passengers and their belongings were offloaded at the first low tide – requiring every horse and cart in the neighbouring area. The *Great Britain* was wedged onto the reef, and it seemed there was no way to shift her: the crew had already offloaded tons of coal but to no avail. Their next hope was the high tide on 28 September, which they hoped might lift her off the reef. The day came, but with a fierce storm that battered the ship violently; Captain Hosken moved the ship further onto the beach – it seemed the only option.

A weaker vessel might have been destroyed by the crash, and certainly by the storms, but the damage caused to the *Great Britain* was only superficial. Yet when Captain Hosken reported

senger liner

the situation back to the Great Western Steamship Company in Bristol, they simply wrote her off. Brunel was enraged – but was too busy with his railways to get away to Ireland, so he left Claxton in charge. Breakwaters were erected around the stranded ship, but they were simply washed away.

Finally in December, Brunel got time enough to visit the *Great Britain*. He was both angry and wounded to see his masterpiece lying abandoned like a vast hunk of scrap metal. He summoned his energies – and those of the people around him, including Claxton and Hosken – to build a defence around the ship. It was incredibly difficult work, as they tried to stave off the battering power of the sea. Brunel designed a defence consisting of brushwood bound into faggots; these would then be speared through with iron rods to secure them into the ground. The end result would be a thick wall that might break the force of the waves through the winter; in the spring, he hoped, they might move her.

Brunel went back to London, leaving Claxton in charge of the work. He wrote to him:

*. . . the finest ship in the world . . . is lying like a useless saucepan kicking about on the most exposed shore that you can imagine, with no more effort or skill applied to protect the property than the said saucepan would have received on the beach at Brighton . . . As to the state of the ship, she is as straight and as sound as she ever was, as a whole . . . It is beautiful to look at, and really how she can be talked of in the way she has been, even by you, I cannot understand. It is positively cruel; it would be like taking away the character of a young woman without any grounds whatever.*[102]

But Claxton soon complained that the faggots would not stay put, and were washed away by the sea as fast as they were built. In reply to this, Brunel wrote to Claxton again, one of his most fierce letters: *You have failed, I think . . . from that which causes nine tenths of all failures in this world, from not doing quite enough . . . I would always impress upon you one principle of action which I have always found very successful, which is to stick obstinately to one plan (until I believe it wrong), and devote all my scheming to that one plan . . .* [103]

Claxton duly tried again, and this time succeeded. The faggots protected the ship through the winter, and in the spring the water was pumped out of her, so that the bottom of the ship could be raised and repaired. Finally on 27 August 1847 there was a tide strong enough to lift the *Great Britain* up off the reef and out of Dundrum Bay, from where she was towed back to Liverpool.

Brunel had saved his great ship – but only for a while. The salvage cost sank the Great Western Steamship Company, after only ten years of business and the production of just two ships. In April 1848, the *Great Britain*'s furniture and fittings were sold at auction. The ship itself – which had cost £125,555 to build – was sold for £18,000 in 1851.

The *Great Britain* was transformed into an emigrant carrier, delivering 15,000 to Australia in 24 years. In 1845 and 1855 she was chartered by the British Government to transport troops to the Crimean War, and in 1856 she carried the first ever English cricket team to tour Australia. By the late 1870s, she was no longer fit to carry passengers and was converted to carry Welsh coal to San Francisco. But in 1886 she was wrecked off the Falkland Islands, where she became a coal and wool storage hulk until 1937. In 1970, she was eventually returned to Bristol, where she has been restored.

But the incident did not blight Brunel's reputation; the *Great Britain* was recognised as a truly original design, if overambitious. Brunel was at the height of his powers, he was recognised as a great engineer of singular vision and talent. And he was famous. By 1845, at the age 39, he had already achieved many of the 'chateaux d'Espagnes' that he had dreamed of in his youth.

Years of relentlessly pursuing his individual schemes had paid off. Now that Brunel's ferocious determination was coupled with the confidence of his successes, he was about to go too far, and make the greatest technical blunder of his career.

# Brunel Falls out of Love with Railways

In 1844, Brunel was inspired to begin yet another extraordinary project. In September of that year he visited Kingstown (now Dun Laoghaire) near Dublin with Daniel Gooch and a group of other renowned engineers to see the operation of a railway that dispensed entirely with steam locomotives. The coal-eating fires blazing in the vast boilers were gone, and instead the force moving the carriages along the track was just air pressure.

The 'atmospheric railway' at Kingstown was causing great excitement. The one and three-quarter mile track was essentially a pneumatic pipe with a stationary pump at one end; five minutes before a train was scheduled this was used to expel the air from the pipe. The atmospheric pressure then drove a piston up the pipe; the piston was coupled to a carriage above, which travelled with it. The hole in the pipe for the coupling would be kept air-tight with a leather valve sealed with grease, which ran the length of the pipe. While the trains themselves were free of steam engines, they were needed to power the pumps. The return trip was driven by gravity alone.

The original inventor of the system was George Selhurst, who in 1799 patented a method for transporting goods and mail at high speed through an iron tube; the system had been developed for rail use in 1838 by Samuel Clegg (a gas engineer) and the shipbuilding brothers, Jacob and Joseph Samuda, who together had patented the design for the valve and additional machinery.

This new method of rail transport caused great excitement in the mid-1840s, when conventional railway lines were spreading across Britain. Railway Mania had taken a firm hold. Between 1845 and 1848, Parliament passed 650 Railway Acts, allowing for the construction of almost 9,000 miles of track.[104] Interest in railway shares was booming and there was plenty of enthusiasm for a new type of railway.

At this time, Brunel was not the only one looking for an alternative to steam, which was widely perceived to be both dirty and dangerous. What's more, it seemed that the atmospheric system would provide a means of drawing carriages up steep hills – at Kingstown, the average speed on an incline was 30 mph – which was still an impossibility for steam locomotives.[105] It also promised to be cheap.

Brunel himself had several new lines; he was now Engineer to the Cheltenham & Great Western Union Railway; the Wiltshire, Somerset & Weymouth Railway, (extending south from Bath); and the South Devon Railway (extending the GWR into the West Country). It was on this last line that Brunel decided to use the atmospheric system, all the way from Exeter to Penzance. He would begin by constructing a 15-mile section of single track from Exeter to Teignmouth.

Certain problems with the atmospheric system might have been immediately anticipated – for instance, the long leather valve was an inevitable weak point; keeping it airtight was bound to be a problem. And there was potential difficulty in the fact

The development of the atmospheric railway inadvertently turned an unsuspecting student into the fastest man on earth. Frank Ebrington, a trainee engineer (and son of a Regius Professor of Dublin University) was preparing to make a test run on the Kingstown-Dalkey atmospheric line. He had just sat down in the motive carriage when quite suddenly it was sucked away without its train. The much-maligned and usually tardy atmospheric system fleetingly achieved great speed, as Ebrington was whisked from Kingstown to Dalkey in just one and a quarter minutes – an average speed of 84 mph.[106]

that the carriage was under the control of an engineman in a pumping station up to 3 miles away – sometimes it didn't reach the end and had to be pushed; on other occasions it overshot the track, since the handbrake onboard was no match for the piston's power.[107]

The Stephensons and Daniel Gooch believed that these problems made the Atmospheric Railway impracticable, but Brunel would not be warned off it: he was utterly convinced of his own ability to push an unconventional system through – as he had done with the GWR – whatever the doubts of others. Besides, Brunel was not alone in backing the Atmospheric Railway – in addition to the Kingstown line, in London the renowned engineer William Cubitt was using it on a five-mile track from New Cross to Croydon.

But Brunel was so busy, it seems, that he never really thought the project through. When he was called before a Parliamentary Select Committee on 4 April 1845 to justify the system, his answers were vague and he waved away the details. When he was asked how the line would be constructed he replied:

*The whole system of working a line with the atmospheric apparatus requires a great deal of consideration and requires many new contrivances and I do not think I have at all completed, to my own satisfaction, all the details . . . I think I see my way clearly to effect them but I should still hope to effect many improvements.*[108]

It was unsurprising then, that Brunel changed the specifications of the railway half way through its construction, changing from a 13-inch diameter pipe to 15 inches, which then demanded more engines to be built to increase the power to the pumps. Since the airtight pipe was incredibly expensive to lay, Brunel attempted to save money by laying only a single line, with passing points – but this meant that the volume and speed of traffic would be hopelessly limited. The line was heavily delayed when the first section finally opened on 13 September 1847 (an extension to Newton Abbott opened on 10 January 1848).

At first, the South Devon Atmospheric Railway was a great attraction; people came to marvel at it. But just one month after the railway opened, the problems began. The main concern was the leather valve, which had to be sealed with a grease of some sort. They tried a lime soap composition, but that hardened on exposure to the air, so next they tried a mixture of soap and cod-oil; that worked better but got sucked into the pipe when the valve opened.[109] The extra exertion on the engine due to the leaking air meant that the whole system was underpowered and slower than anticipated.

But it wasn't just keeping the valve airtight that was a problem; the oxhide leather itself proved to be a difficult material: in winter it froze rigid, and in the summer (when it was more palatable) there were reports that rats chewed it away.

By the beginning of September 1848, the Atmospheric Railway was closed. The Directors instructed its conversion to conventional locomotive haulage from 10 September, and Brunel – who had spent £433,991 on what was now seen as a vainglorious enterprise – had to explain himself to the South Devon Railway shareholders, whose money he had spent. On this occasion, he waived his fee – and stayed away from South Devon.

The problems weren't exclusive to Brunel's line. Cubitt's Croydon line also suffered problems with the valve and closed in 1847; the Kingstown line lasted until 1854. But in France, the Paris à St-Germain atmospheric line which ran the 1.4 miles from Bois de Vezinet to St-Germain, had a much longer life, from 1847 to 1860; it was this short distance (and hence low speed) that made the Paris line more viable. Perhaps the basis of this, Brunel's greatest blunder, was the fact that he was so busy at this time that he didn't check the suitability of the atmospheric system for what he hoped would be a faster and longer line.

The failure of the Atmospheric Railway was an embarrassment for Brunel, and it came at a bad time, when severe difficulties were emerging in other projects. The same Railway Mania that had prompted Brunel to take up the atmospheric system was also causing problems with the GWR. The proliferation of railway lines created an increasingly dense network of lines; and railway companies competed to expand their territories by linking up to others. For the GWR, who had a distinct broad-gauge system that was incapable of connecting with the rest of the country, this was an increasingly urgent issue. Brunel had created the problem of a bi-partisan railway system, and it now had to be resolved: a choice had to be made between narrow- or broad-gauge.

There was no obvious winner. The narrow gauge had been around for longer, but the broad gauge had advantages in performance. Now that Brunel had improved the lay of his track, and Gooch had created an enviable fleet of locomotives, the GWR trains were the fastest in the world. In 1844, the GWR opened their line to Exeter, extending their reach far into the southwest of England. On the first run, on 1 May 1844, the 194-mile trip was completed in 4 hours and 40 minutes, an unrivalled performance.[110] By the next year, a GWR journey from Paddington to Exeter took only five hours, including time taken for stops – these were the world's first express trains.[111]

Brunel was made Engineer to the South Wales Railway in 1844, and this gave the GWR company opportunity to expand the broad gauge into Wales (where profitable coal contracts might be won). In that same year, two more schemes were proposed to use the broad gauge: on the Oxford, Worcester & Wolverhampton Railway and the Oxford & Rugby Railway. This expansion into the Midlands angered the narrow gauge companies in the southwest and the Midlands in particular, who felt their territory was being invaded by the broad gauge. It was not just a matter of competition; the clash of the gauges was becoming a significant logistical problem. At Gloucester, where the two gauges met – the narrow-gauge Birmingham & Gloucester line entered the city

from the north, while the broad-gauge line from Swindon came from the south – 'through' passengers were forced to leave their standard gauge train to cross the platform for a broad gauge train, to continue their journey. For goods traffic, the delay was up to four to five hours, as it was manhandled from one train to another. By 1845, there were ten of these chaotic junctions of different gauge.[112]

The fierce rivalry between broad and narrow gauge companies soon became a matter for public debate in newspapers, and pamphlets were even distributed bearing information on the 'gauge war'. It had become a national issue. In July 1845, a Royal Commission was appointed to investigate the matter, consisting of Sir Frederick Smith (previously Inspector General of the Railways); George Biddell Airey (Astronomical Royal, from the Greenwich Observatory) and Peter Barlow (Professor of Mathematics at the Royal Military Academy, Woolwich, who had advised Stephenson on the mathematical limitations of gradients and curves in railway tracks).

On 6 August 1845 the proceedings began; 48 witnesses – the great and the good of railway experts – would be examined over 30 days. When Brunel was called before the Commissioners on 25 October, he was characteristically combative.

Brunel claimed that the existence of different gauges was good for 'competition', and that the break of gauge was, in the spirit of that competition, inevitable. He continued to argue for the technical superiority of the broad gauge – he claimed that amongst its technical advantages was the fact since the carriages could fit more seats, fewer carriages were required on each train – which in turn meant that less fuel was required to move them. Gooch calculated that a narrow gauge train had a rolling resistance of 40lb per ton at 60 mph, while a broad gauge train had only 18lb per ton.[113] Of course, the opposition – the narrow gauge – represented by its stalwart supporters George Bidder and Robert Stephenson, challenged these figures. With supreme confidence and a fondness for action,

The Illustrated London News published this picture to show a view of the chaotic 'b

uage,' from wide to narrow tracks at Gloucester

Brunel offered to settle the debate with a series of trials pitching the performance of the broad gauge directly against the narrow. The idea was accepted and the trials were set for December.

But Brunel had been somewhat rash to suggest the trial: the narrow gauge locomotives had undergone several recent revisions and improvements, but no new broad gauge locomotive had been built since 1842. So on behalf of the broad gauge, Gooch selected *Ixion* (built in 1841) from the 'Firefly' class to pitch against 'Engine A', a brand new Stephensonian 'Long Boiler'.

The locomotive *Lightning*, on broad gauge tracks

The broad-gauge *Ixion* (with her 7ft diameter wheels) would run 53 miles on the Paddington to Didcot line, while her rival, Engine A (running on wheels of 6ft 6in diameter, but with a much more powerful boiler) would run the 44 miles from Darlington to York. *Ixion* went first. The future of Brunel's broad-gauge empire

rested on her performance. She made three trips on the course, with varying loads. Hauling an 80-ton train, she averaged 53 mph, and carrying less she was even faster.

Now, it was the turn of Engine A, for the narrow gauge. George Bidder added certain modifications to stack the odds in her favour, using pre-heated water in the boiler, and starting the timing from a flying start.[114] But his efforts were wasted: Engine A reached a maximum speed of 53 mph – at which she even came off the track – hauling a load of only 50 tons. The older – but better-designed – *Ixion* had won the day for Brunel, Gooch and the broad gauge.

So when the commissioners reported to Parliament early in 1846, Brunel and his colleagues were surprised that it was in favour of the narrow gauge. The Commissioners acknowledged the superior speed of the broad gauge track and the benefits of the larger carriages, but reasoned that there were already 1,901 miles of narrow gauge, and only 274 miles of broad gauge, and they were worried by the break of gauge, already such a problem at Gloucester.[115] They saw the need for a standard track and ruled: 'If it were imperative to produce uniformity, we should recommend that uniformity be produced by an alteration of the broad to narrow gauge.'[116]

Brunel, however, would not be beaten – nor silenced. He wrote a fifty-page refutation of the Commissioners' findings, *'Observations on the report of the Gauge Commissioners'* pointing out the errors, as he saw them, in their findings. He then printed it up as a pamphlet and used it to lobby Parliament, making sure that every MP had a copy. His persuasive powers worked yet again. When the Gauge Act of 1846 was passed, it stated that the narrow 4ft 8½ inches gauge was the legal gauge of Britain, but contained a clause allowing for the broad gauge to continue.

Yet, with or without the clause – or even the Commissioners' Report – the days of the broad gauge were numbered. Just as the

THE BURIAL OF THE "BROAD-GAUGE."

Linley Sambourne's cartoon of the ghost of Brunel lamenting the burial of his broad gauge, *Punch* 1892

commissioners had argued, the narrow gauge already had a greater spread over Britain, and the broad gauge could not catch up – Brunel was simply too late. He had pursued his ideal railway against commercial sense; the tide had already gone with the narrow gauge. (Fortunately, Brunel did not live to see the conversion to narrow gauge which began – at great expense to the GWR Company – from the 1860s, and completed on 20 and 21 May 1892 with the conversion of Brunel's entire main line from Paddington to Penzance.)

Despite the 1846 ruling in favour of the narrow gauge, Brunel's extraordinary contributions to railway design were not exhausted. At the same time that his engineering abilities were being questioned by the detractors of the broad gauge and the critics of the atmospheric system, Brunel was starting out on the creation of a railway engineering work that many would call his masterpiece – the Royal Albert Bridge.

The merits of wider versus standard gauge size are still debated by engineers. It's probably fair to say that Brunel did not need to resort to a dramatically different gauge size to improve speed and running on the lines: his better-designed track, and improved locomotives could have achieved that alone.[117] But, recent high-speed trains have employed wider gauge – for example the TGV in France and the Shikansen lines of the 'bullet trains' in Japan. In Britain, wider freight and high-speed trains are more easily accommodated on Brunel's lines, which have bigger tunnels.

The extension of the South Devon Railway into Cornwall demanded that at some point the River Tamar must be crossed. The Tamar is a wide river, and on a line from Plymouth to Falmouth there were few places where an easy crossing could be made. Brunel settled on Saltash where the river narrowed to 1,100 feet, with steep sides. Brunel's first design was for a series of timber spans (one of 225 feet, and six of 105 feet) set 70 feet above high water mark.[118] But the Admiralty insisted on having a clear headway of 100 feet and so Brunel had to come up with another plan; he eventually arrived at a central pier in mid-stream, with two spans of 465 feet.[119]

Such a design depended entirely on the structure of the riverbed

– but finding that out wouldn't be easy; the water was 70 feet deep over a thick layer of mud. Divers were sent down but brought back little reliable information. Brunel needed a device in which the riverbed could be examined at depth, and for hours on end. In 1848, a huge wrought iron cylinder (85 feet long and 6 feet wide) was sunk into the riverbed to act as a caisson.[120] The water was pumped out, and from inside the giant tube trial borings were made in 35 different positions to map out the rock under the riverbed, until Brunel found the most solid foundation for his pier.

It was complicated and risky work. Brunel was fortunate to be working simultaneously on a smaller bridge – at Chepstow over the river Wye (for the South Wales Railway) – that he could use

John Lucas's portrait of a conference of engineers for the Britannia Bridge. Brunel is on the far right

as something of a trial-run for the bridge over the Tamar. The Chepstow Bridge involved the use of caissons and another pressing design issue, namely how to make iron bridges sufficiently strong. Robert Stephenson's cast-iron Dee Bridge, had recently collapsed killing five people.[121]

Stephenson (lucky to escape a manslaughter charge) had moved on to a wrought iron box-girder structure, which he successfully employed at the Britannia Bridge over the Menai Straits; here the train ran through the 'box', which gained strength from the rigid structure. Brunel developed a different approach: he also favoured wrought iron,[122] but decided that semi-circular section forms were best able to withstand compression. Rather than make these the beams at the base of a bridge, Brunel realised he could make them run across the top as trusses, which would – when in compression – support a structure (namely the railway track) below.

At Chepstow, he designed parallel tubular trusses (circular in cross-section) to act as the support for two longitudinal iron girders, which carried the track. The girders were hung on suspension chains from either side of the trusses.

Although the bridge at Chepstow had a main span of only 300 feet (plus three land spans of 100 feet extending beyond the tubular design) he realised that its core design – using the tubes in compression – might be transferred to Saltash.

Here, he applied the same principle, but incorporated an incredibly ingenious design.

Most bridges are 'open systems' that is, they draw on support outside their own structure to keep them stable and upright – for example, the 'tie-back' chains that run from the Clifton Suspension Bridge to the land on either side of the gorge, which prevents the weight of the deck and suspension chains from collapsing inwards. But the Royal Albert Bridge is, exceptionally, a closed system. Here the weight of the deck and the chains is counterbalanced by the compression in the tubular trusses (this time oval in cross-section) arching overhead, without any need to draw support from the surrounding land.

But before building of this structure had even begun, work on the bridge came to a firm stop. In 1847, the furious track-laying and expansion of the railways that had triggered the gauge war stopped; the money had run out. Finally, the railway bubble had burst. Stock prices crashed; thousands of individuals were bankrupted and even some banks were ruined. In November of that year, hundreds of the staff from the Swindon factory were released; those who kept their jobs paid 3.5 per cent of their wages to a fund to support the unemployed. Brunel contributed £100 to this fund, and Gooch gave £50.[123]

This was also a turning-point for Brunel. Although he was yet to complete the Royal Albert Bridge – amongst his finest work of all on the GWR – he recognised that the glory days of the railways were over. In his ambition to create the finest railway in England, Brunel had endured the embarrassing failure of the Atmospheric Railway, and defeat in the gauge war. Now, as railway stocks plummeted, there was an ugly scramble for opportunistic investment. Brunel was disgusted and disillusioned by it.

*Here the whole world is railway mad. I am really sick of hearing proposals made. I wish it were at an end ... it would suit my interests and those of my clients perfectly if all railways were stopped for years to come.*[124]

He began to retreat, and re-kindled one of the 'chateau d'Espagnes' of his youth: that of designing and building his own house in the country, surrounded by a great garden. Shortly after the financial collapse of the railways, Brunel made his first investment in that dream – on visiting the town of Barton, near Torquay, he found the perfect site, with views across Babbacombe Bay to the sea. Here, he might retire. Brunel had taken his eye off work for once – but as usual, his ambitions were grand.

He drew up plans for an elaborate house and garden. William Burn – the pre-eminent country house architect of the time – was appointed to design the house, in the style of a Loire valley chateau. For the garden, Brunel called in W A Nesfield, the gardener at Eton, and probably the country's premier tree expert – he had set out Regent's Park and was advisor to the Royal Botanical Gardens at Kew.

Brunel's drawings reveal that he was involved in planting each and every tree; he kept meticulous charts, plotting the growth and girth of each tree and bush, year on year. Watcombe became his obsession and his release. Yet, it was never finished – in fact, at the time he died only the foundations were built. But from 1847 onwards, Watcombe provided him with a dream, a place to escape from his soured experience of the over-commercialised railways.

The Royal Albert Bridge over the river Tamar at Saltash, under construction, 1859

By 1851, the fortunes of the railway companies were still low and there was insufficient money to finish Brunel's bridge at Saltash. So, in April 1852, Brunel made a radical alteration to his design, changing it from double track to single, which instantly cut

£100,000 off the cost. Finally the building of the structure could begin. Work started with the masonry piers, and again there was the problem of how work could proceed deep underwater. Since the work was extensive and Brunel could not risk leaks, he realised that an ordinary coffer dam would not do. So he came up with a new design of a wrought iron main tube – 35 feet wide – containing another tube within it – in the form of a diving bell – in which the masons worked.

In the 4-foot space between the diving bell and the outer tube, 30 men worked to excavate the 16 feet of mud of the river bed. This outer space was pressurised, to prevent water seeping through into the inner tube, one of the first uses of a pressurised caisson in Britain. This 'great cylinder', which weighed over 300 tons, was built on the riverbank before being floated on the tide and then lowered into position (a process which took two weeks).

By the end of 1856, the pier was completed and the iron trusses could be added. These were also fully prefabricated on shore, and then floated on the river on pontoons, from where they were jacked up the piers to their final position, 30.5m above water level. Each truss weighed 1,060 tons and on 1 September 1857, 300,000 people watched the tricky task of lifting the western truss into position. Still the eastern truss had to be raised and the chains and supports added. It was 1859 before the bridge was finally opened.

Brunel's fortunes with the railways had been truly mixed – from embarrassment over the atmospheric system to rivalry and enmity over the gauge war. But the Royal Albert Bridge was a triumph which still today marks Brunel's unique and elegant contribution to railway design.

# International Affairs

Following the collapse of the 'Railway bubble' in 1847, there was a slump in Brunel's fortunes – as there was in the entire railway industry. But while the railways faltered in Britain, elsewhere they were just getting started, and Brunel began to receive requests for his expertise from around the globe.

In Ireland he constructed lines from Cork to Youghal,[125] and from Dublin to Wicklow,[126] although progress was slow due to the Potato Famine that began in 1845. In Italy, between 1845 and 1848 he was engineer to a short line in Tuscany, named the 'Maria Antonia Railway'. In the 1850s he consulted with India (remotely, from England) over the construction of a 150-mile line for the Eastern Bengal Railway; and in so doing he was one of those engineers who facilitated British Imperialism in India. The Colonial Office to Australia also consulted Brunel, asking for his advice on the building of lines to Melbourne and Williamstown, which would carry people and goods to and from the gold rush.

The British Empire was expanding rapidly – powered by British industry and innovation – and there was new enthusiasm for international trade . This brought fresh opportunities for Brunel back in England, far beyond advising on a few railway lines.

In 1849, Henry Cole of the Royal Society of the Arts, Manufactures and Commerce had an idea for an exhibition that would be unlike anything ever before seen in England. 'The Exhibition of the Works of All Nations' – known as the 'Great Exhibition' – would be unprecedented in scale and revolutionary in its international scope. Cole enlisted the patronage of Prince

An engraving of Isambard Kingdom Brunel , 1850

Albert, who liked the idea and the opportunity it offered to promote peace between nations; so he appointed a Royal Commission to make this great feat happen, the active officers being Henry Cole and John Scott Russell.

When the Commission created a Building Committee to choose the design, Brunel was one of three engineers invited to join; along with Robert Stephenson and William Cubitt. In January 1850, they joined two architects and two aristocrats on the committee.

They didn't have long to select and construct the building; the Exhibition was scheduled for the next summer, 1851. Designs were invited from the public, but when the committee examined all 245 received, none were deemed suitable. By the summer of 1850, they were still without a design. So the Committee decided to have a go themselves, and came up with a large brick building with a vast cast iron dome, 150 feet high and 200 feet in diameter (this last extravagance was Brunel's contribution). The public were saved from this dark and oppressive building by a new design with entirely opposite properties of light and delicacy. Joseph Paxton was a gardener at Chatsworth and had drawn inspiration for this design from the greenhouses there, and from the structure of the giant water lilies he grew, with their strong arching bifurcations on the underside of the lilypads. It was accepted and work on its construction in Hyde Park began at once.

Paxton's design of a prefabricated structure of cast iron and vast glass panels meant that despite its vast size – six times that of St Paul's Cathedral – it could be made and assembled in the remaining few months before the opening of the Exhibition in May 1851. The magazine *Punch* sarcastically dubbed it the 'Crystal Palace'; the name stuck and became an affectionate one.

The Commissioners gave Brunel a second responsibility, that of chairman of the jury of Class Vii, on Civil Engineering. As ever, he voiced his opinions clearly, and expressed a prejudice against all electric machines, calling them 'toys' (this was in spite of the fact that the electric telegraph had been used on railway communications since 1838[127]). He also let it be known that he disapproved of monetary prizes for the exhibitors, believing that participation should be reward enough. Brunel's own achievements were represented by Gooch's latest, most imposing locomotive, *The Lord of the Isles.*

Over six million visitors visited the Exhibition to see more than 13,000 exhibits from all over the world, in the six months it stood at Hyde Park.[128] It was a great success.

For Brunel, the Great Exhibition was particularly fruitful: the Crystal Palace building had provided him with inspiration for another project: Paddington Station. Since the opening of the terminus at Paddington, it had functioned with only four platforms and a station in the form of a wooden-roofed train shed.[129] As the volume of traffic increased in the early 1850s, the need to expand and replace the existing station became increasingly pressing.

On 13 January 1851, Brunel wrote to Matthew Digby Wyatt, who was secretary to the Royal Commission for the Great Exhibition, but also a renowned architect, to engage him on the project:

*Now, such a thing will be entirely metal as to all the general forms, arrangements and design; . . . it is a branch of architecture of which I am fond, and, of course, believe myself fully competent for; but for detail of ornamentation I neither have time nor knowledge, and with all my confidence in my own ability I have never any objection to advice and assistance even in the department which I keep to myself, namely the general design.*

The resulting iron and glass building displayed the legacy of the Crystal Palace; Brunel even used the same contractors, Fox, Henderson & Co. Three great wrought-iron roof spans were supported by cast-iron columns, with delicate decorative ironwork by Digby Wyatt. The new station was 700 ft long and 240 ft wide, and had ten tracks, five of which were platform lines, while the other five were for rolling stock. Brunel's beautiful design remained unchanged for 40 years, until 1878 when additional platforms were added. The station has since been extended, but Brunel's roof remains.

Brunel's Great Western Railway Terminus at Paddington Station, 1854

Besides inspiring Brunel's design for Paddington, the Great Exhibition provided another great opportunity for Brunel: he made contact with John Scott Russell, an acquaintance which would form the basis of Brunel's next great project – possibly the grandest of them all – the *Great Eastern*.

Brunel had known Scott Russell for many years; they had first met in Bristol in 1836, at the BAAS meeting where Dionysius Lardner had (erroneously) pronounced Brunel's plans for a transatlantic steamship impossible. Scott Russell had sprung to Brunel's defence, and a mutual respect developed between them.

Scott Russell was a Glaswegian, and something of a prodigy. He started out on a career in the church but became fascinated with the first Newcomen steam engines at the Carntyne mines, and abandoned the church in favour of engineering. By the age of just 24 he was made Professor of Natural Philosophy at Edinburgh University. He then turned his hand to naval architecture where he established the 'wave-line' principle for shipbuilding in 1836; this aimed to reduce the ship's resistance in the water, so that it could reach a desired speed with the least possible consumption of power.

So when, just a few months after the Great Exhibition closed, Brunel had an idea for a new steamship of unprecedented size, it was to Scott Russell that he turned. What Brunel had in mind was a ship of such vast proportions that it would have the capacity to carry enough coal to steam all the way to Australia without taking the time to re-fuel on the way. (The availability of coal to steamships was a significant problem; local supplies were often of poor quality, and if British supplies were stockpiled abroad they were charged import duty.)

The Great Exhibition had revealed the wealth and resources in Australia, and now waves of people clamoured to escape the financial hardship of Britain in the 1840s, to cash in on the gold rush on the other side of the world. Brunel realised he could build a ship to take these emigrants all the way there.

On 25 March 1852, Brunel had made a sketch of a steamship in his diary and written underneath it: *Say 600ft x 65 ft x 30ft.*[130] In this rough drawing lay the kernel of years of hard work, frustration and conflict for Brunel, but also for John Scott Russell. As he sketched the 'Great Ship', Brunel can have had no idea that after all his close encounters with death, this would be the project that would kill him.

The dimensions Brunel had sketched out were for a ship six times larger than any afloat. Such a ship would benefit from an economy of scale, and would be both fast and economical, requiring less crew than on several smaller ships. But she would require more powerful machinery than ever used before. Brunel realised she

John Scott Russell photographed next to the *Great Eastern*

would need more than one propulsion system. Since twin-screws were still highly experimental, he settled on the combination of screw and paddle wheel propulsion, with ancillary sail power.[131] The inclusion of the paddle wheels meant that the ship would also be fit to reach Calcutta, where the waters of the River Hoogly were too shallow for a screw propeller to function. She would be unlike anything the world had ever seen before.

Towards the end of 1852, Brunel took his plan to Scott Russell, and his old ally Captain Claxton. (This time, Thomas Guppy was not involved, since he had moved to Italy in 1849.) Scott Russell examined Brunel's plan, and made his own calculations to see if such a ship was even possible to build. He calculated that it would have a displacement of 20,000 tons, and would require 850 horsepower to travel at 14 knots.[132] But he believed it was possible.

At Scott Russell's suggestion, they approached the Directors of the Eastern Steam Navigation Company (ESNC), who had recently lost the mail contract for the Far East to the Peninsular and Oriental Steam Navigation Company. They were now looking for one or two large ships to provide an alternative means of cashing in on that profitable route; Brunel's ship promised to compete with the fast clippers that currently dominated the route, as she did not have to spend time in port refuelling.

On the day Brunel had arranged to meet the ESNC, he was ill and Scott Russell went in his place. Even though this distanced Brunel's maverick reputation from the project, the outlandish scale of the idea was enough to cause some of the committee members – including the chairman – to resign. Yet, the ESNC accepted the proposal. Brunel was officially appointed engineer to the project and he proceeded to gather tenders to build the ship.

Although Brunel had estimated the cost of building his great ship at around £500,000, Scott Russell offered a suspiciously low tender of £275,200 for the hull. Oddly, this doesn't seem to have been questioned and in May 1853 the tender was accepted. Scott Russell would build the hull, and the paddle engines, while James Watt & Co would build the screw engines. The construction of the *Great Eastern* would consume the next seven years of the lives of Brunel and Scott Russell; but they didn't yet know it would reduce their alliance to bitter enmity and result in near-calamity for them both.

Neverthless, the template for this unfortunate ending was laid out from the start. Both Brunel and Scott Russell regarded the project as their own; Brunel because it was his idea, and Scott Russell because he was charged with the actual building of the ship. It was a difficult grounding on which to begin the building of this extraordinarily novel vessel. Brunel was accustomed to having complete control over a project, and even where he had co-operated in the past – on the *Great Western* and *Great Britain* for example –the project had still run to Brunel's overall direction and design.

Scott Russell was an experienced shipbuilder and expected to be able to interpret Brunel's designs according to his own knowledge – Brunel regarded this as plain interference. Brunel was always covetous of his projects and this – his most monumental so far – was impossible for him to let go. This was in spite of the fact that he had agreed for Scott Russell to build the ship in his London shipyard at Milwall.

While Brunel gave over the building of the hull and the engines to Scott Russell and James Watt, he kept a close eye on the details. He would spend days examining the plans, and frequently went to Scott Russell's yard to inspect the progress. Yet – as ever – Brunel increased his workload by taking on other projects. Soon after work began on the Great Ship, Brunel under-took one last important international venture, when he played a part in the Crimean War.

The British involvement had begun on 28 March 1854 when Britain and her allies declared war on Russia. By early 1855, there was already an undeniable crisis for the British troops. Not only were the army's methods of warfare outmoded, having changed little since the Battle of Waterloo in 1815, but soldiers were dying in their thousands.

When Florence Nightingale arrived (with her party of 38 nurses) at the army hospital at Scutari, in Turkey, she found that only one death in six was attributable to war wounds; the rest were caused by disease. As the army prepared for the Siege of

Sevastopol, there were only 11,000 British troops left; a greater number, 12,000, were in hospital.[133] The hospitals themselves were disastrously equipped; the only access to Scutari was from the sea, so patients were brought by boat, and then carried on stretchers up steep painful slopes. Once inside, there was no drainage system, and the water supply was polluted – it was found to flow through the rotting carcass of a horse.[134]

An artist's impression of Florence Nightingale in a ward at Scutari

Nightingale received more obstruction than help from the British military and doctors, who felt that her actions and demands for reform were an insult to their professionalism. So she went to instead to the press; the editor of *The Times*, John Delane, picked up her story of ill-treatment of British soldiers, and it quickly became a national scandal.

Like the army, the government was reluctant to change practices at the whim of an outsider and a woman at that. At the forefront of the government resistance to Nightingale was the Permanent Under Secretary at the War Office, who Nightingale described as: '. . . a dictator, an autocrat irresponsible to Parliament, quite unassailable from any quarter, immovable in the midst of a so-called constitutional government'.[135] This man was no other than Ben Hawes, Brunel's old friend and brother-in-law. Hawes decided to enlist the help of Brunel to build a hospital that would show Nightingale what could be achieved without her interference.

On 16 February 1855, Hawes wrote to Brunel to ask him to design an improved hospital for the British Army in the Crimea, that could be built quickly in England, then shipped to the next war zone, for immediate on-the-spot assembly.

When approached by Hawes, Brunel temporarily swallowed his dislike for authority and immediately set to work on the design. He created a plan that fully incorporated Nightingale's recommendations on ventilation, hygiene and sanitation, and pre-sented it to the War Office just six days later.

Brunel's design was for a 1,000-bed hospital and it was ingen-ious. The building was entirely pre-fabricated (like the Crystal Palace); once erected it formed a series of wooden huts, large enough to allow for 1,000 cubic feet of air space per patient that – along with a ventilator fan which introduced humidified air into each unit – would limit the spread of disease through contact. The timber roof was covered with tin to reflect away the heat of the sun, and flush toilets and hand-basins would prevent contamination from effluent.

A site was chosen for Brunel's hospital at Renkioi, on the southern shores of the Dardanelles. With astonishing speed, the parts were built and transported on five separate ships to Renkioi, where they arrived in May. By 12 July it was ready to admit its first 300 patients and by 4 December had reached its capacity of 1,000 beds. By this time, the campaign in the Crimea was nearing its end. But in the remaining days of the war up to January 1856, the hospital treated 1,331 men of whom only 50 died – a 4 per cent fatality rate compared to 42 per cent at Scutari (although, admittedly, since Renkioi was further from the Crimean Peninsula, most of its patients were convalescent rather than recently wounded).[136]

Brunel's hospital had only a short life at Renkioi, but Florence Nightingale was delighted with it, and it became an important model for future hospitals, as well as a prototype for simple pre-fabricated buildings.

Brunel had come back from his depression after the decline of the railways, and widened his reputation by expanding his work beyond railways, and by taking on international projects of fantastic diversity. And he had started the construction of the *Great Eastern* – the most mammoth engineering task of his career – which would now dominate his life until its end.

# The Great Ship

The *Great Eastern* was the ultimate, extravagant conclusion of Brunel's dream of creating a network of transport that was capable of reaching around the globe. Brunel determined that his ship would not only be on a mammoth scale, it would also be a fantastic spectacle of luxury. The first-class cabins and public rooms were to be fitted out with the opulence of a luxury hotel, replete with chandeliers, thick carpets and mahogany furniture upholstered in buttery velvet.

His final design gave the *Great Eastern* a length of 211 metres (693 ft), a width of 37 metres (120 ft), and a depth of hull of 18 metres (58 ft), creating an overall displacement of 22,500 tons. The paddle wheels were 56 feet in diameter, while the 24-foot screw weighed 36 tons alone. Brunel made space for 4,000 passengers by using two new devices: skylights to illuminate the inner cabins and air-trunks to provide them with ventilation. These features enabled Brunel to place cabins deep inside the ship, rather than following convention and placing them on the deck. With this design, Brunel increased deck space. Owing to the deck's great size – 680 feet long and 120 feet wide – and the gaslights that cast their golden light across it, it would be nicknamed 'Oxford Street'. The ship's mammoth proportions soon led to her becoming known as 'The Leviathan'. She would be the largest steamship built for the next 40 years (until the *Lusitania* in 1907).

Building a ship of this size – and to Brunel's uncompromising specification – would take a lot of money. The Eastern Steam Company needed to raise at least £800,000 or 40,000 shares before work could start. Brunel's reputation for having overspent on previous projects didn't help matters. Charles Geach, the Rotherham-based ironmaster, who supplied much of the ironwork for the ship (also a friend of Scott Russell's) provided a good deal of the funding. Brunel managed to persuade the railway contractors Samuel Peto and Thomas Brassey[137] to invest and took a large stake in the Company himself. Finally the money was raised.

But there was an immediate – and rather portentous – threat to the future of the *Great Eastern*. On 10 September 1853, a fire broke out at Scott Russell's shipyard. The flames began to engulf the yard, and the large quantities of timber within it, throwing out a great light. The Fire Brigade raced to put it out, charging towards the source of the light. But – it was reported in *The Times* – the fierce light had deceived them into thinking the fire was on the south side of the river, near Deptford, rather than on the Isle of Dogs. By the time the fire engines reached Scott Russell's yard, an hour later, the fire had taken hold. Scott Russell's yard was consumed, causing £140,000 worth of damage. Unfortunately, less than half of this value was insured; Scott Russell's buildings were destroyed along with his timber, his plans and works in progress.

The future of the *Great Eastern* was secured only by Charles Geach, who covered the costs of the fire. (Geach would continue to help out Scott Russell, by taking company shares as payment for iron when Scott Russell could not afford cash.)

From the outset, Brunel was anxious to exert his control over Scott Russell, and when the contract was drawn up, dated 22 December 1853, Brunel ensured that it was stated: *All calculations, drawings, models and templates which the contractor may prepare shall from time to time be submitted to the Engineer for his revision and alteration or approval.*[138] (Since Brunel refused to have a Resident Engineer, 'the Engineer' was himself). What's more, Brunel informed Scott Russell that he would be paid as railway workers were paid – in monthly instalments, according to how much work had been done. Scott Russell protested – shipbuilders were usually paid lump sums at fixed intervals – but Brunel got his way.

At last, in the spring of 1854, work could begin. Scott Russell's yard was too small for the mammoth proportions of the Leviathan, so he rented Napier's yard at Milwall. Even there, conventional construction was impossible. The size of the ship meant that she could not be launched by the stern from a slipway as other vessels

The *Great Eastern* under construction at Milwall dockyards

were, since she would immediately run aground on the riverbank opposite. So she would have to be constructed parallel to the Thames, and launched that way too, when the time came.

The area in which she was built was strengthened with more than 1,500 timber piles, each 24 feet long, which were driven into the ground and then filled-in with concrete. Iron rails were then laid on the launching ways. Two giant timber cradles were erected for the ship to be built in, and on their lower faces were iron strips, running parallel to the axis of the ship.[139] Brunel believed that the two iron surfaces would reduce friction when it came to launching the ship.

Brunel had designed his ship from first principles – and insisted that Scott Russell abandon his preconceptions. Ignoring the conventions of wooden shipbuilding, he had considered what would work best for an enormous form at sea. He came up with a revolutionary design, which would be adopted as a mainstay

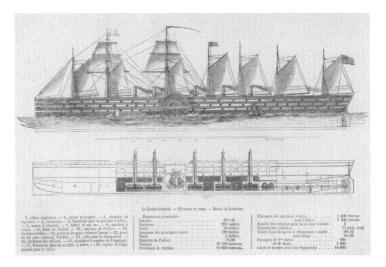

Cross-section giving dimensions of the *Great Eastern*

of modern shipbuilding. The most important feature was a double hull consisting of an outer and inner skin of iron, 2 feet 10 inches apart. By joining the two skins together with bulkheads, a honeycomb of closed-off cells would be created; Brunel saw that each box-like cell would offer strength without weight – just like the box-girders used in Stephenson's Britannia Bridge construction.

He insisted that every part of the ship's structure must contribute to her strength:

*The principle of construction of the ship is in fact entirely new, if merely from the rule which I have laid down, and shall rigidly preserve, that no materials shall be employed at any part except at the place, and in the direction, and in the proportion, in which it is required, and can be usefully employed for the strength of the ship, and none merely for the purpose of facilitating the framing and first construction.*[140]

Brunel's next innovation was to build the hull of standardised parts; every plate was the same size, as was every bar and every rivet. The *Great Eastern*'s hull was pieced together as an enormous patchwork of iron. First, the transverse bulkheads and inner skin were built, followed by the longitudinal bulkheads, and the webs to which the outer skin was riveted. Since Brunel had rejected a crane as too costly, every iron plate – 10 feet by 2 feet 9 inches – had to be manually hauled up and then riveted into place. In all, the ship required over 30,000 wrought-iron plates and three million rivets, every one of which had to be driven by hand. Riveting was done in gangs of five, in which there were two riveters, one 'holder-on', and two 'bash-boys', one of who heated the rivets, and the other inserted them into the hole.

The thunderous sound of 200 of these gangs constantly riveting, constantly hammering metal must have been deafening – they worked up to 12 hours a day, six days a week. While the outer skin was riveted, the 'holder-on' and his boy would often spend whole days, even weeks, working in the faint flicker of candlelight between the two skins, enveloped by the banging.

There were certainly many people killed or injured. Amongst those who fell to their death was a workboy who fell head-first from the ship's side, and was impaled on an upright iron bar. 'After he was dead, his body quivered for some time', one witness said. One man was unlucky enough to be killed on a short visit to the site, he: 'in prying about, was bending over the head of a pile, when the monkey came down, flattening his head'.[141]

For enduring these risks, a skilled man could earn 30–40 shillings a week. Workers had few rights – after all, if you complained there were hundreds of others, ready to replace you. As the ship grew, she was covered by a colony of 2,000 human workers, crawling over her and between her two skins.

Brunel (third from the left) and a group of figures demonstrate the scale of the steamship

Brunel would have been horrified to know that even early on in the ship's construction, Scott Russell was getting himself – and the *Great Eastern* – into deep financial trouble. The start of the Crimean War in March 1854, had already pushed up the prices of iron. Then, in October 1854 Charles Geach died; and so Scott Russell lost his financial safety valve. Scott Russell saw no other solution but to mortgage his yard – but, realising this would jeopardise the future of the Great Ship, he kept this a secret.

Animosity between Brunel and Scott Russell was already growing. Brunel was already very suspicious of Scott Russell, and an article published in *The Observer* in November 1854 brought things to a head for the first time. The unsigned article attributed the design of the *Great Eastern* primarily to Scott Russell, and stated that Brunel only 'approved' the project. When Brunel read the article he was enraged that Scott Russell should steal his glory, and immediately assumed that Scott Russell was the author.

Scott Russell responded to Brunel's accusations in a letter: '1st, I have as much reputation as I desire or deserve. 2nd I think it much wiser to be just than unjust. 3rd I would much rather preserve your friendship (which I think I possess) than filch your fame (if I could) and forfeit your friendship which I should.'[142]

But Brunel's jealousy was not abated; another source of contention between Brunel and Scott Russell developed – how to launch the ship once the hull was finished. Not only had Brunel suggested an unconventional sideways launch but he now stated that the ship was at risk of being grounded in the river by the usual 'free launch' and should undergo a 'controlled' launch instead. Scott Russell quite reasonably opposed Brunel's plans as he had never seen a ship launched in this way and he saw it as a costly endeavour.[143]

A launch date of October 1855 was set. But in April of that year, Scott Russell suffered another fire in his yard. The *Great Eastern* was unscathed, but Scott Russell was pushed further into debt. Brunel conceded that the launch date must be deferred.

Relations between the two men only grew worse through the summer of 1855 as Brunel persisted in his plans for a controlled launch, and wrote to ask Scott Russell for the weight and other proportions of the ship, for his calculations. On 27 September, Scott Russell replied with various figures, including the weight –

and a protest about his lack of payment. Brunel found fault with Scott Russell's weight for the ship – perhaps he assumed that Scott Russell was withholding the information to block his plans for a controlled launch – and wrote a furious reply:

*How the devil can you say you satisfied yourself as to the weight of the ship when the figures your clerk gave you are 1,000 tons less than I make it or than you made it a few months ago – for shame – if you are satisfied then I am sorry to give you trouble but I think you will thank me for it. I wish you were my obedient servant, I should begin with a little flogging.*[144]

Brunel's possessiveness over the Great Ship exceeded anything he had shown for previous projects, and this near-paranoia was fuelled by Scott Russell's relaxed management style. Brunel was infuriated by what he saw as a lax attitude to his precious 'Great Babe', as he called the ship. For his part, Scott Russell had years of experience of working with his men, and allowing them some latitude in their interpretation of his instructions and design; he put his trust in them. But this would not do for Brunel who insisted on monitoring every development – and had given himself licence to do so in the contract.

So, when in January 1856 Brunel calculated that 2,500 tons of iron plate had gone missing from Scott Russell's yard, he immediately jumped to the worst conclusion. He wrote a letter to the Board of the Eastern Steam Navigation Company, and laid the blame squarely with Scott Russell.

*I make the quantity in the yard 1,400 tons but this would still leave 800 or 900 tons to be accounted for and I am totally at a loss to suggest even a probable explanation . . . Mr Russell, I regret to say, no longer appears to attend either to my friendly representations and entreaties or to my own formal demands and my duty to the company compels me to state that I see no means of obtaining proper attention to the terms of the contract otherwise than by refusing to recommend the advance of any more money.*[145]

For Scott Russell, already in debt, this was a fatal blow. Martin's Bank refused further credit and on 4 February 1856, the Scott Russell Shipbuilding Company ceased trading. As the bank took possession of the premises, Scott Russell's secret mortgaging of his yard, years previously, became public. Now, he was forced to lay off many of his men. Work on the Great Ship came to a stop, and the half-built hull, usually clanging with the industry of thousands of men, was abandoned and silent.

Now, Brunel had the upper hand and he took the opportunity to shake things up – but he was heavy-handed about it. He angered Yates, the yard manager, by telling him to lock up the

A photograph taken shortly before the first attempted launch of the *Great Eastern*

stores to prevent any pilfering; Yates (who was also the Company Secretary) took this badly and complained of being undermined. Brunel next tried to hire Scott Russell's assistants, Dickson and Hepworth, as his own, but was outraged when they wanted a commensurate salary.[146] However, it was not so easy to get rid of

Scott Russell, who was desperately keen to finish the job. Finally, after a great deal of haggling with Brunel and the Board, it was agreed that Scott Russell should finish the construction of the hull and the steam paddle engines.

Martin's Bank eventually recognised that the Eastern Steam Company had a valid need to use the yard, and agreed to lease it to them until August 1857. A new date for launch was set for spring 1857. Work on the Great Ship resumed, with Brunel emphatically in charge, but more paranoid than ever. This period was extremely difficult for him – he placed himself under enormous pressure to control every aspect of the *Great Eastern*'s construction; he kept up a draining antagonism to Scott Russell, and at this time he was still engaged on other projects – most notably the construction of the Royal Albert Bridge. On top of all of this, it seemed that Brunel was suffering from some sort of physical illness.

Nonetheless, as the Great Ship began to take shape, excitement about this fabulous construction began to spread through the people of England, and even into Europe. In April 1857, *The Times* wrote:

'Where is man to go for a new sight? We think we can say. In the midst of that dreary region known as Millwall, where the atmosphere is tarry, and everything seems slimy and amphibious, where it is hard to say whether the land has been rescued from the water, or the water encroached upon the land . . . a gigantic scheme is in progress, which if not an entire novelty, is at as near an approach to it as this generation is ever likely to witness'.

The ship was almost finished by June, but the launch date had to be postponed once more, to 5 October, due to the ongoing question of how the ship would actually enter the water. The date arrived, and still the Great Ship was not ready for launch; the yard was seized by the creditors. To regain access to work on the ship the Eastern Steam Company was forced to agree to pay huge fees. To try to keep the costs of these fees

Brunel's iconic and most famous photographic portrait

down, the new launch date was fixed for much sooner than Brunel would have liked; 3 November, when there would be a large 'spring' tide.

Brunel had prepared for his controlled launch by piling the slipway with huge square oak piles, over 12 inches in cross section and 20 to 38 feet long, at intervals of 5 feet.[147] On the river there would be four 80-ton hand-winches on barges, which were attached to the ship by chains. At the bow and the stern, chains would run to pulleys on moored barges and then back to steam-winches on the riverbank. In addition to this, there would be one hydraulic ram at the bow and one at the stern. Once the ship was moving, Brunel planned to control its launch with chains connected to two braked drums, 9 feet in diameter and 20 feet long, which in turn were operated by hand. Due to the financial pressure to clear the ship from the yard, Brunel had no chance to test his method of launching, in which he had to shift the 12,000-ton hull over a distance of 200 feet to the water. In the days approaching the launch, Brunel barely left the yard, and hardly slept.

Brunel wanted silence for his launch, and wrote explicit instructions to everyone involved in the launch to this effect. Even on 3 November, the day of the launch, he had no idea that in their desire to recoup some of the money lost during the ship's extended and troubled construction, the ESNC had sold 3,000 tickets to the public to watch the launch like a performance. The press – who had taken a great interest in the project throughout – built up the launch into a great public event. There were visiting dignitaries, including the Comte de Paris and the ambassador of Siam, and bands played in the streets outside.

Brunel was thrust into a circus of publicity, of which he wanted no part. He ignored the ceremony in which the daughter of the chairman of the ESNC, Miss Hope, cracked a bottle of champagne against the ship's side, and christened her *Leviathan* –

John Scott Russell, Lord Derby, Brunel and Henry Wakefield at the unsuccessful launch of the *Great Eastern*

they had even got the ship's name wrong; she was formally registered as the *Great Eastern*.

As Brunel climbed to a platform above the crowds, from which he would issue his signals for launch, there was no chance of the silence he wanted. The checking chains were released and the first pressure was applied. For several minutes nothing happened. Then, suddenly, the bow cradle shifted 3 feet. The brake lever was applied to the forward checking drum, and at the point, the stern moved forward several feet, to the delight of the cheering crowd. This movement pulled the chain of the rear checking drum tight, and sent the winch handle spinning. The men operating it were taken by surprise and several of them were sliced by its fierce movement and some were even flung high into the air. One of them, John Donovan, aged 74, died of his injuries.

The launch descended into chaos and was aborted. It had been an unremitting disaster, and a public one at that. But Brunel tried again as soon as he could. The second launch attempt took place on 19 November. Having decided that the winches on the barges in mid-river were ineffective, Brunel had moved them into the yard; he also added two more hydraulic presses. This time, the ship moved only 1 inch.

Brunel made two more attempts on 28 and 29 November, and despite problems with the equipment, these were more hopeful; by the 30th, the ship had moved 33 feet towards the water. It seemed Brunel's controlled launch might be possible after all. But when a cylinder burst in one of the hydraulic presses, and the bitter weather of December and January set in, hope was lost again.

The watching public were fascinated by this technological saga and when someone placed an advert for solutions, there were hundreds of responses. Amongst the most ingenious were ideas for using the vibrations of an army of tramping soldiers to shake the ship on its way, or similarly to use the blasts of cannon blows or gunpowder.

Meanwhile, the press grew impatient and their fascination with the *Great Eastern* started to turn to criticism and even ridicule.

'Mr. Brunel has not been altogether un-familiar with failures; but no failure of his ever did so much to lower the reputation of English engineers as the launch of the Leviathan. Having first, by the construction of that enormous vessel, concentrated the attention of the world upon him, he has now presented to it the greatest and most costly example of professional folly that was ever seen . . . it was, in our judgement, an altogether unnecessary display of self-confidence in Mr. Brunel to build the ship where she is, particularly as the narrowness of the river and the populousness of its banks rendered a rapid launch extremely dangerous.'

*The Mechanic's Magazine*,
Tuesday December 15th 1857

Stephenson, Scott Russell and Brunel before the final launch of the *Great Eastern*

Brunel grew increasingly depressed. He discussed his plans for the launch with his friend and erstwhile competitor, Robert Stephenson, and decided that the best strategy would simply be to push harder, by acquiring more hydraulic presses. He got hold of as many of the devices as he could.

Another launch date was set for 30 January 1858. Using the force of 18 hydraulic rams, the *Great Eastern* at last reached the water's edge. That night, Brunel stayed on board with his son Henry, too excited to sleep. At dawn the next morning, Brunel saw there was a strong tide, and took his chance.

After two hours of pushing, the *Great Eastern* finally took to the Thames with Brunel, Henry and Mary on board. This time, there were no crowds and no bands – just a handful of onlookers. The cost of the launch had been extraordinary – over £120,000 – and much of this was Brunel's own money. Not only had Brunel invested his own capital in the ship but he had worked for no pay from Eastern Steam Company, and paid his assistants from his own pocket. But the cost to Brunel's health had been even greater. His heroic tenacity had ensured the safe launch of the world's largest ship, but Brunel would pay dearly.

# Tragedy at Sea and at Home

After three months of effort, the *Great Eastern* was finally on the water. But still she wasn't finished. She was now floated to Deptford for the final stage in her fitting-out. Brunel was absent for most of the process; his health was worsening and on his doctor's advice he spent from May to September 1858 with his wife Mary, in the South of France. Although he was meant to be recuperating, he could not resist the temptation of working on plans for the East Bengal Railway.[148]

When Brunel returned in September 1858 he was in for a shock. The fitting-out of the ship had not progressed at all; the Eastern Steam & Navigation Company was so heavily in debt that they had no money left to carry on. The cost of the hull had far exceeded initial estimates: already more than £750,000 had been spent, plus £95,000 owing for materials.[149] Efforts to raise the £172,000 necessary to continue working on the ship had come to nothing. Now, the Directors of the ESNC talked of selling Brunel's Great Babe. Some of those Directors still wanted to get rid of Brunel himself.

A solution was found by creating a new company, amongst a group of the Directors. The new 'Great Ship Company' then bought the ship for a paltry £160,000 on 25 November 1858; shares were allotted to shareholders in the ESNC according to their original distribution. Brunel was appointed Engineer for the new company, and he threw himself into the role wholeheartedly, attending to every minute detail from the rigging to the crew. But his progress was marred by his failing health; the trip to France had not cured him of his illness. Now, Brunel's doctor, Dr Richard Bright, made his diagnosis. Brunel was suffering from nephritis, an inflammation of the kidneys that causes high blood pressure, sometimes leading to kidney failure.[150] In Brunel's case it was chronic; his incessant smoking of cigars and relentless work cannot have helped his condition. The doctor ordered him to spend the winter in Egypt, where the warm weather might ease his symptoms.

Brunel was not happy to leave his Great Ship, now that her completion was so close. Before he left, he detailed his specification for the fitting, and gave instructions that – after the experience of Scott Russell's haphazard accounting – all contracts for the fitting-out should be clear and binding.

Brunel left for Egypt in December 1858. In January 1859, in Brunel's absence, the Directors of the Great Ship Company appointed the major contract for fitting-out the ship. It went to none other than Scott Russell who, once more, offered a very low tender. Although this decision may have disappointed Brunel, the work went well under Scott Russell who, after all, had invested years of work building the hull and paddle-wheel engines of the ship.

Brunel's travelling companions were his wife Mary and Dr Parkes, superintendent of the hospital Brunel had designed at Renkioi. They collected Brunel's son Henry at Geneva on the way out, before taking a paddle-steamer along the Mediterranean. They spent Christmas in Cairo with Robert Stephenson, who was also suffering an incurable illness. They then sailed down the Nile at a leisurely pace, visiting the ancient sites on their way. Henry kept a diary that reveals that Brunel was – predictably – not entirely at rest during the trip. He busied himself with calculations along the way, and chartered a boat to navigate the rapids above Aswan.

The return journey took them through Italy and Europe and they arrived back in England in May 1859. Brunel had missed Prince Albert himself opening the Royal Albert Bridge, by just a few days. He was taken to see the completed bridge, but was not fit to stand, so he lay on a couch on a carriage truck, which was pulled across the bridge by a locomotive. Although his trip to Egypt had provided a rare opportunity for some relaxation, Brunel was still weak. Nonethelesss, he continued to visit the *Great Eastern* almost daily, where the work of fitting her out continued largely under Scott Russell's direction.

Finally, at the end of July, the *Great Eastern* was replete with all engines, and the fine furnishings of which Brunel had dreamt when he first imagined her. On 8 August, a great banquet was thrown on board the ship, attended by MPs, and members of the House of Lords. They dined under the chandeliers in the extravagant rococo saloon. But Brunel was too weak to go, and Scott Russell took centre stage (and all the glory) in his absence.

On Monday 5 September, however, Brunel felt well enough to board the ship and give her an inspection. He chose his cabin for the maiden voyage, and stopped to have his photograph taken. Leaning on his stick, he looks markedly frailer than the bulldog-like man photographed by Robert Howlett just two years before, in 1857.

The last photograph of Brunel, taken on board the *Great Eastern*

Two hours later, he collapsed with a stroke. He was taken to Duke Street in his carriage, with the utmost care. He was conscious throughout the journey and once at home, he issued instructions from his bed for the imminent voyage.

On Wednesday 7th, the *Great Eastern* finally slipped her moorings and sailed down the Thames. This initial part of the journey would be something of a trial, since neither the paddle-wheel engines nor the screw engines had been given proper sea trials. As yet, the ship had no licence to carry passengers, so there were only 50 or so people on board: members of the press, specially-invited guests and the crew.

In Brunel's absence, overall command of the ship had theoretically passed to Captain Harrison, but he lacked a thorough knowledge of the ship's novel devices, and was somewhat pushed aside by the engineers and contractors all trying to see how their particular engine was working. There was no real sense of hierarchy or command across the ship.

On Friday 9 September, the *Great Eastern* set off down the English Channel with great smoothness and majesty. Several passengers strode along the decks, enjoying the air. As she passed the Dungeness Light, just after six in the evening, there was a sudden and enormous explosion. The first of the five funnels – 100 feet high and 6 feet in diameter – shot upwards on a plume of steam and smoke; much of the deck and the forward saloon went with it. Steaming hot water burst into the paddle-engine boiler room, scalding the stokers in its path; they emerged on the deck with their skins slack and boiled white. Debris from the explosion rained down on the ship, and there was wild confusion as passengers and crew ran for their lives.

One quick-thinking crew-member realised immediately the cause of the accident: a stopcock had mistakenly been turned off, which allowed pressure to build in the water jacket surrounding the forward funnel. At once, he sent a greaser to the second funnel, to release the stopcock and prevent the same thing happening again.

Once the chaos was over, the damage was assessed. Five stokers died of their burns, and twelve more people were badly injured. The explosion had ripped a great hole in the ship but she had carried on unaffected, drawing power from the remaining engines, just as Brunel had designed her to. A lesser ship would have been destroyed. The *Great Eastern*'s incredible resistance had been proved, but at a terrible price.

Brunel lay at home, unaware of the disaster – excitedly waiting for news of his ship's first voyage.

The next day, the *Great Eastern* drew into Portland Harbour in Weymouth, where an inquest was begun almost immediately, to establish the cause of death of the five stokers, and secondly to investigate the general safety of the ship. Proceedings began on Monday 12 September in Weymouth town hall, where the witnesses, and a jury of 15 men were assembled by the coroner for the District of Weymouth. Scott Russell was unable to attend and the inquest started slowly.

But on the following days, as the witnesses were called, very

An engraving from the *The Illustrated London News* of the collapsed funnel on the deck of the *Great Eastern* after the explosion

little was explained of how the crucial stopcock in the foremost water jacket had come to be turned off. Without Brunel on board there was no single person in charge; the chain of command was broken and the management of the ship had descended into a fragmented chaos. No one would admit that the stopcock was under his charge.

Scott Russell claimed that by the time he was on board, his responsibilities were over; he had merely made the engines, and stood on the ship in a supervisory role only. But several witnesses said they saw him standing on the bridge with Captain Harrison, giving orders. What's more, as the ship had departed, Brunel had issued instructions for the engines to be properly tested – and surely Scott Russell had a responsibility for executing these commands; especially since the team from James Watt & Co had accepted similar responsibility for the screw engines. However, it was true that Scott Russell had no overall control of the ship, and undoubtedly had its success and its safety at heart.

Just like Scott Russell, every witness had a reason for eschewing responsibility for the stopcock. It was impossible to pinpoint anyone for blame, and so a verdict of accidental death was recorded.

Brunel was still lying at home at Duke Street when he heard of the accident. He was distraught. His Great Babe had malfunctioned on her first outing and five men had died as a result. When he heard the news, he was already a weak man. Each day after that, he waited eagerly for any news from the inquest. But he did not survive for long. He died at 10:30pm on Thursday 15 September, six days after the explosion. He was aged just 53. Whether it was the shock that killed him is not known.

As for the *Great Eastern*, after three weeks of repairs and modifications (the replacement of the funnel, and the removal of the feed-water tanks) she steamed on to Holyhead. There, she was ceremoniously welcomed by dignitaries, but it was deemed by the Great Ship Company too late in the year for her to continue with a voyage across the Atlantic. It was agreed that Captain Harrison would take her to Southampton, to wait out the winter. But there another disaster befell the ship.

One day in January, Captain Harrison, together with a small crew, took a sailboat out to reach the Great Ship. During the short journey, a storm blew up suddenly. Despite the efforts of Harrison and his men, the sailboat overturned; Harrison struggled, but he could not right it. Within minutes, Harrison was drowned along with the coxswain and the ship's boy. A curse seemed to hang over the ship, until she finally reached New York on 27 June 1860. At last, she was received as a triumph; the whole country was electrified by the sight of this extraordinary feat of engineering. But she was unable to fulfil her true potential.

The Great Ship Company was almost bankrupt, and could not afford to finance the run to Australia for which the *Great Eastern* had been built. So instead, she continued to do the transatlantic run, even though it was now adequately served by smaller ships. On a crossing in August 1862, she struck a rock off Long Island, which tore open an 83-foot gash in the hull. It was thanks only to the inner steel skin that she kept afloat; most other vessels would have sunk straight away (as the *Titanic* would in 1912). But the repair costs were so great that they

In 1865, the *Great Eastern* was bought by the Great Eastern Steamship Company and modified as a telegraph-cable laying ship, in which capacity she laid the very first trans-Atlantic telegraph cable (1,400 nautical miles). She laid four more lines before 1874. She was then refitted to transport American visitors from New York to the 1867 Paris Exposition. In 1869 she returned to cable-laying, until she was laid up at Milford Haven in 1872. In 1884, she was bought for £26,200 for use as a floating music hall in Liverpool. After four years, she was sold for just £16,000 to a firm of shipbreakers in Birkenhead, who took over two years to break her up (twice as long as anticipated).

In New York crowds gathered to watch the Great Eastern dock, it would be thirty years before any ship rivalled her size

finally bankrupted the Great Ship Company and they were forced to sell her in July 1865.

The *Great Eastern*'s scale and remarkably resilient cellular structure were ahead of her time, but she was never a commercial success.

Brunel was buried at Kensal Green Cemetery on 20 September 1859. His funeral was attended by a large number of friends, family and fellow engineers. Thousands of railwaymen lined the route to the cemetery to pay their respects to this diminutive giant of their industry.

In November of the same year it was decided that a monument should be dedicated to Brunel's honour. 'I.K.Brunel 1859' was placed over each arch of the Royal Albert Bridge. The following year, 1860, a group within the Institution of Civil Engineers decided to honour Brunel by finally completing his first big project: the suspension bridge at Clifton. One of the main proponents was John Hawkshaw – who had so vehemently opposed Brunel's broad gauge.

At the time, Hawkshaw was building a railway bridge into Charing Cross, which required the dismantling of Brunel's footbridge, the Hungerford suspension bridge. So Hawkshaw took Brunel's original chains and incorporated them into the Clifton Suspension Bridge. It was opened on 8 December 1864, with some changes to Brunel's original design (slightly scaled down, and without the decorative panels on the towers) but in the same setting and with the same span.

Daniel Gooch wrote in his diary of Brunel's death:

'By his death the greatest of England's engineers was lost, the man with the greatest originality of thought and power of execution, bold in his plans, but right. The commercial world thought him extravagant; but although he was so, great things are not done by those who sit down and count the cost of every thought and act.'[151]

Today, many British cities have streets named after Brunel, and there is even a university that bears his name. His influence was so great, that it is difficult to live in Britain without encountering – or benefiting from – his work in some way. He not only had an extraordinarily clear vision of engineering, but a determination that enabled him to carry through anything to which he set his mind. He had a magical ability to draw people into the excitement of his vision, and make them believe in it too. For a supposedly hard-headed engineer, he had a romantic attachment to ideals and dreams that made him inspirational where others were merely effective.

# Notes

1 Andrew Mathewson and Derek Laval, *Brunel's Tunnel . . . and where it led* (Brunel Exhibition Rotherhithe: 1992) p8.

2 Celia Noble, *The Brunels, Father & Son*, (Cobden Sanderson, London: 1838) p11.

3 Noble: *The Brunels*, pp13–17.

4 L T C Rolt, *Isambard Kingdom Brunel* (Penguin, London: 1989, 4th ed), p28.

5 Rolt, *Brunel*, p30.

6 Noble, *The Brunels*, p24.

7 Now 98 Cheyne Row.

8 Adrian Vaughan, *Isambard Kingdom Brunel, Engineering Knight Errant* (John Murray, London: 3rd ed, 2003) p6.

9 Vaughan, *Engineering Knight Errant*, p5; other authors, for example, L T C Rolt, have argued that Brunel mastered Euclid when he was just six years old.

10 Noble, *The Brunels*, pp35–46.

11 Noble, *The Brunels*, p42.

12 Noble, *The Brunels*, p42.

13 Quoted in Vaughan, *Engineering Knight Errant*, p8.

14 Vaughan, *Engineering Knight Errant*, p8.

15 Noble, *The Brunels*, p45.

16 This connection was possibly made through Sophia's family, since her grandfather was Thomas Mudge, the great English clockmaker.

17 Years later, Isambard would use one of these 'inverted V' engines in his ship the *Great Britain*.

18 Isambard Kingdom Brunel, Journal, Tuesday 10 May 1825, hereafter IKB/Journal.

19 Noble, *The Brunels*, p51.

20 At the point at which Trevithick's tunnel was abandoned, there was only 200 feet further to go, out of a total 1,200 feet.

21 Tim Bryan, *Brunel, The Great Engineer* (Ian Allan Publishing, Surrey: 1999), p11.

22 IKB/ Journal, Wednesday 2 March 1825.

23 Mathewson and Laval, *The Tunnel*, p18.

24 Angus Buchanan, *Brunel, The Life and Times of Isambard Kingdom Brunel* (Hambledon and London, London: 2002) p24.

25 Richard Beamish, *Memoir of the Life of Sir Marc Isambard Brunel* (1862), p241, quoted in Buchanan, *Brunel*, p24.

26 Vaughan, *Engineering Knight Errant*, p21.

27 Rolt, *Brunel*, p55.

28 Isambard Kingdom Brunel, Private Diary, 13 October 1827, hereafter IKB/ Priv Diary.

29 Richard Beamish's claim in his memoir of Marc Brunel; discussed by Vaughan, *Engineering Knight Errant*, p24.

30 Rolt, *Brunel*, p59.

31 IKB/ Priv Diary, 8 February 1828.

32 IKB/ Priv Diary, 6 December 1831, p218.

33 IKB/ Priv Diary, 13 October 1827.

34 IKB/ Priv Diary, 21 November 1827.

35  IKB/ Priv Diary, 21 November 1827.

36  IKB/ Priv Diary, 6 April 1829.

37  IKB/ Priv Diary, 13 October 1827.

38  IKB/ Priv Diary, 4 November 1827.

39  IKB/ Priv Diary, 6 and 7 May 1828.

40  The idea of building a bridge across the Avon Gorge originated in 1754, with a bequest in the will of Bristolian merchant William Vick, who left £1,000 invested with instructions that when the interest had accumulated to £10,000 it should be used for the purpose of building a stone bridge between Clifton Down and Leigh Woods, both of which were barely populated at the time. By the 1820s Vick's bequest was nearing £8,000, but it was estimated that a stone bridge would cost over ten times that amount. An Act of Parliament was passed to allow a wrought-iron suspension bridge to be built instead, and tolls levied to recoup the cost.

41  There is disagreement over why IKB went to Bristol; whether he went there before the competition to convalesce, or whether he went purely for the competition. But in Brunel's diaries there is no direct mention of going to Bristol to convalesce, just an off-hand reference to a visit to Redcliff a suburb of Bristol.

42  Telford's bridge crosses the Menai Sraits, joining Anglesey to North West Wales. It was opened on 30 January 1826, following the Act of Union of 1800, which increased the need for transport to Ireland. Holyhead was one of the most convenient terminals for Dublin.

43  Quoted in Rolt, *Brunel*, p 72.

44  IKB/ Priv Diary, 22 April 1832, p306.

45  Bryan, *Brunel, the Great Engineer*, p19.

46  The letter is printed in its entirety in Noble, *The Brunels*, p109.

47  Qouted in Rolt, *Brunel*, p87.

48  IKB/ Priv Diary, 10 January 1833.

49  IKB/ Priv Diary, 3 December 1831.

50  IKB/ Priv Diary, 8 April 1829.

51  Jack Simmons (ed), *The Birth of the Great Western Railway, Extracts from the Diary and Correspondence of George Henry Gibbs*, (Adams & Dart, Bath: 1971), p3 of Introduction.

52  IKB/ Priv Diary (1832–1840), 21st February 1833.

53  Quoted in Vaughan, *Engineering Knight Errant*, p46.

54  IKB/ Priv Diary (1832–1840), 21 February 1833.

55  IKB/ Priv Diary (1832–1840), 22 February 1833.

56  Bryan, *Brunel the Great Engineer*, p34.

57  Quoted in Rolt, *Brunel*, p107.

58  Rolt, *Brunel*, p112.

59  There is an apocryphal story that this distance in turn, was inherited from Roman chariots whose wheels were set about five feet apart, see Tim Bryan, 'The Battle of the Gauges: Brunel's Broad Gauge' in Eric Kentley (ed) *Isambard Kingdom Brunel, Recent Works* (Design Museum, London: 2000) p40.

60  IKB/ Priv Diary (1832–1840), 26 December 1835.

61  IKB/ Priv Diary (1832–1840), 26 December 1835.

62  Rolt, *Brunel*, p125.

63  Rolt states that Sophy's autograph book also includes the names of Brahms, Chopin, Joseph Joachim and Nicolo Paganini the great violinists; Ignaz Moscheles the pianist.

64  IKB/ Priv Diary (1832–1840), 14 April 1836.

65  Quoted in Rolt, *Brunel*, pp130–1.

66 Rolt, *Brunel*, p126.

67 Noble, *The Brunels*, p135.

68 Noble, *The Brunels*, pp134–5.

69 Quoted in John Pudney, *Brunel and his World* (Thames and Hudson, London: 1974) pp52–3.

70 Rolt, *Brunel*, p140.

71 Bryan, 'The Battle of the Gauges' in Kentley (ed) *Brunel: Recent Works*, p48.

72 Although the Box Tunnel was the longest *railway* tunnel in the world at the time, it was not the longest tunnel as Brunel had claimed; the Sapperton tunnel on the Thames and Severn Canal was about 500m longer and more than 50 years older.

73 Bryan, *Brunel, the Great Engineer*, p68.

74 Bryan, 'The Battle of the Gauges', in Kentley (ed) *Brunel: Recent Works*, p48.

75 Although the *Savannah*, a 350-ton coaster had made the first transatlantic crossing in May 1819 (taking 29 days 11 hours to travel from Savannah Georgia to Liverpool) for most of the journey the power came from the ships sails, and the steam engines were only used occasionally, so this cannot really be classed as a transatlantic steam crossing.

76 Quoted in Bryan, *Brunel the Great Engineer*, p76.

77 According to Vaughan, *Engineering Knight Errant*, p90.

78 Vaughan, *Engineering Knight Errant*, p93.

79 IKB's letter is quoted in full in Rolt, *Brunel*, pp153–4.

80 Letters to Thomas Guppy, Letter 5, 11 May 1838.

81 Bryan, 'The Battle of the Gauges' in Kentley (ed), *Brunel: Recent Works*, p46.

82 Diary of George Henry Gibbs, 6 October 1838, in Simmons (ed) *The Birth of the Great Western Railway*, p54.

83 Diary of George Henry Gibbs, 14 December 1838 in Simmons (ed) *The Birth of the Great Western Railway*, p61.

84 Diary of George Henry Gibbs, 29 December 1838 in Simmons (ed) *The Birth of the Great Western Railway*, p63.

85 Quoted in *Bryan, Brunel, the Great Engineer*, p45.

86 Diary of George Henry Gibbs 10 January 1839 in Simmons (ed) *The Birth of the Great Western Railway*, p64.

87 In *Brunel, the Great Engineer*, p55, Bryan cites recent research that it may not have been the storm of 1839 that blew away the supports; rather, they were removed under Brunel's instructions in early 1840.

88 Quoted in Vaughan, *Engineering Knight Errant*, p121.

89 Bryan, 'The Battle of the Gauges' in Kentley (ed), *Brunel: Recent Works*, p48.

90 IKB/ Priv Diary (1832–1840), 26 December 1835.

91 Celia Noble went on to write the biography: '*The Brunels, Father & Son*' about Marc and Isambard.

92 Pudney, *Brunel & His World*, p49.

93 Vaughan, *Engineering Knight Errant*, p157.

94 Andrew Lambert, 'Brunel and the Screw Propeller' in Kentley (ed) *Brunel: Recent Works*, p104.

95 Quoted in Andrew Lambert, 'Brunel and the Screw Propeller' in Kentley (ed) *Brunel: Recent Works*, p106.

96 Rolt, *Brunel*, pp266–7.

97 Rolt, *Brunel*, p283.

98 Buchanan, *Brunel*, p178.

99 Bryan, *Brunel, the Great Engineer*, p90.

100 Pudney, *Brunel and his World*, p84.

101 Apparently, it also occurred to Brunel that the cause of the accident might have been the confusion of the magnetic compass

by the iron hull. A solution for this was not found until Professor William Thomson (later made Lord Kelvin) invented the binnacle, an extensive series of magnets in which the compass was housed, and which counteracted the distorting effects of the hull.

102 Quoted in Rolt, *Brunel*, pp274–5.

103 Quoted in Rolt, *Brunel*, p276.

104 Jack Simmons, *the Railways of Britain*, (2nd ed, London 1968), p17.

105 Rolt, *Brunel*, p216.

106 Rolt, *Brunel*, p217.

107 Bryan, *Brunel the Great Engineer*, p103.

108 Vaughan, *Engineering Knight Errant*, p174.

109 Rolt, *Brunel*, p 224.

110 Rolt, *Brunel*, p195.

111 Rolt, *Brunel*, p195.

112 Bryan, 'The Battle of the Gauges' in Kentley (ed) *Brunel: Recent Works*.

113 Vaughan makes this argument in *Engineering Knight Errant*, p220.

114 Rolt, *Brunel*, p291.

115 Lengths of narrow gauge and broad gauge lines taken from Rolt, *Brunel*, p202.

116 Quoted in Bryan, 'The Battle of the Gauges' in Kentley (ed) *Brunel: Recent Works* p51.

117 Vaughan makes this argument in his book, *Engineering Knight Errant*.

118 John Binding, 'The Final Bridge, The Design of the Royal Albert Bridge at Saltash' in Kentley (ed) *Brunel: Recent Works*, p89.

119 Later reduced to 455ft.

120 Binding, "The Final Bridge" in Kentley (ed) *Brunel: Recent Works* p90.

121 Brunel was called as an expert witness after the collapse of the Dee Bridge, but he was reluctant to testify against his old friend,

Robert Stephenson, and refused to condemn cast iron as a building material.

122 Brunel chose to use wrought iron in his Chepstow Bridge after Robert Stephenson had made extensive investigations into its properties for his Conway and Britannia bridges.

123 Vaughan, *Engineering Knight Errant*, p202.

124 Letter to friend, 1844.

125 Work completed under Brunel's assistant, Hughes, see Buchanan, *Brunel*, p85.

126 Finally opened in October 1855, see Buchanan, *Brunel*, p85.

127 Vaughan, *Engineering Knight Errant*, p229.

128 Brunel helped with its transfer to Sydenham, from 1852, and designed two water towers for the new site.

129 Tim Bryan, *Railway Heritage: Paddington, Great Western Gateway* (Silver Link Publishing, Kettering: 1997), p13 hardback.

130 IKB/ Priv Diary, 25th March 1852.

131 Denis Griffiths, 'The Leviathan, Designing the *Great Eastern*' in Kentley (ed) *Brunel: Recent Works* p116.

132 Vaughan, *Engineering Knight Errant* p231.

133 Rolt, *Brunel*, p288.

134 Rolt, *Brunel*, p288.

135 Quoted in Eric Kentley 'A Turkish Prefab, The Renkioi Hospital' in Kentley (ed) *Brunel: Recent Works* p74.

136 Kentley 'A Turkish Prefab' in Kentley (ed) *Brunel: Recent Works* p81.

137 Vaughan, *Engineering Knight Errant*, p232.

138 Quoted in Rolt, *Brunel*, p 313.

139 Denis Griffiths "The Leviathan, Designing the Great Eastern". in Kentley (ed) *Brunel: Recent Works* p126.

140 Quoted in Denis Griffiths 'The Leviathan, Designing the *Great Eastern*' in Kentley (ed) *Brunel: Recent Works* p118.

141 Deborah Cadbury, *Seven Wonders of the Industrial World* (Harper Perennial, London: 2004) p24.

142 Quoted in Rolt, *Brunel*, p319.

143 Brunel had a correspondence with GW Bull of Buffalo, New York, who had successfully executed sideways launches, but they had always been free launches, not controlled as Brunel's would be.

144 IKB to Scott Russell 2 October 1855. Quoted in Buchanan, *Brunel*, p121.

145 Buchanan, *Brunel*, p121.

146 Vaughan, *Engineering Knight Errant*, p251.

147 Many of these oak piles still remain at the site of Napier's yard, off West Ferry Road, on the Isle of Dogs. Some of the original chains also remain.

148 Vaughan, *Engineering Knight Errant*, p263.

149 Vaughan, *Engineering Knight Errant*, p262.

150 It is also known as Bright's disease, since the same doctor made the connection between the symptoms and kidney dysfunction.

151 Roger Burdett Wilson (ed), *Sir Daniel Gooch: Memoirs and his Diary* (Newton Abbot, 1972).

# Chronology

| Year | Age | Life |
| --- | --- | --- |
| 1769 | | 25 April: Marc Isambard Brunel (MIB) born at Hacqueville, Normandy. |
| 1792 | | MIB is forced to leave Paris due to his royalist sympathies. In Rouen, amongst the loyalists, he meets Sophia Kingdom, daughter of a Plymouth naval contractor, and they fall in love. |
| 1793 | | MIB flees to New York to escape Revolutionaries. He travels through America, becomes an American citizen and is appointed Chief Engineer of New York. |
| 1799 | | 20 January: MIB leaves America.<br>13 March: MIB arrives in England, and develops his designs for block-making machines. He meets Henry Maudsley, who agrees to build them, and then takes the designs to the Royal Navy which accepts them.<br>1 November: MIB marries Sophia Kingdom. |
| 1799–1806 | | MIB's block-making machinery under construction. |
| 1806 | | 9 April: Isambard Kingdom Brunel born at Portsea. |

| Year | History | Culture |
|---|---|---|
| 1769 | Frederick II of Prussia and Emperor Joseph II discuss Partition of Poland. Birth of Napoleon. Birth of the Duke of Wellington. First steam road carriage built in France. | Fragonard, *The Study*. Painter Joshua Reynolds knighted |
| 1792 | French Republic proclaimed: Louis XVI arrested. Outbreak of French Revolutionary War. First domestic gas lighting in England. | Paine, *Rights of Man*, Part 2. Rouget de Lisle, *La Marseillaise*. |
| 1793 | Louis XVI executed. Committee of Public Safety formed in Paris: beginning of the Terror. Great Britain at war with Revolutionary France. Napoleon recaptures Toulon from Royalist rebels. | Canova, *Cupid and Psyche*. David, *The Murder of Marat*. |
| 1799 | Napoleon repulsed at Acre: returns to France and is appointed First Consul. | Beethoven, Symphony No 1 in C Major. Hayden, *Creation* oratorio. |

1799–1806

| 1806 | Napoleon defeats Prussians at Jena and Auerstadt and enters Berlin. 'Continental System', barring British trade from Europe, begins. | Rossini's first opera, *Demetrio a Polibio*, produced. Work begins on the Arc de Triomphe, Paris. |

| Year | Age | Life |
| --- | --- | --- |
| 1821 | 15 | May: MIB incarcerated for debt in King's Bench Prison. He is released in July when the Duke of Wellington issues him with a grant of £5,000. |
| 1822 | 16 | IKB is sent to the Lycee Henri-Quatre in Paris, to finish his education. On his return, he joins his father's drawing office at 29 Poultry, London. |
| 1824 | 18 | 20 July: MIB appointed Engineer to Thames Tunnel. Family moves to Blackfriars. |
| 1826 | 20 | 7 August: MIB taken ill with pleurisy due to poor working conditions in the tunnel; IKB takes control of the Thames Tunnel works. |
| 1828 | 22 | 28 January: Major flooding in the tunnel damages the work and inflicts internal injuries on IKB. Work on the tunnel is halted for seven years. IKB goes to Bristol to convalesce. |
| 1829 | 23 | While in Bristol, IKB enters a competition to design a bridge across the Clifton Gorge; and he wins. |

| Year | History | Culture |
|------|---------|---------|
| 1821 | Death of Napoleon on St Helena Coronation of King George IV. Faraday discovers principles of electromagnetic rotation. | De Quincey, *Confessions of an English Opium Eater*. Constable, *The Hay Wain*. |
| 1822 | Turks invade Greece. Brazil becomes independent of Brazil. George Stephenson builds first iron railway bridge for the Stockton-Darlington railway. | Pushkin, *Eugene Onegin*. |
| 1824 | First Burmese War: British take Rangoon. Death of Lord Byron. Portland cement invented. | Beethoven, Symphony No 9 in D Major. |
| 1826 | End of the First Burmese War. First railway tunnel opened on the Liverpool-Manchester line. | Cooper, *The Last of the Mohicans*. Mendelssohn, Overture to 'A Midsummer Night's Dream'. |
| 1828 | Duke of Wellington becomes Prime Minister. Russia declares war on Turkey. Construction of first US railway, the Baltimore and Ohio, begins. | Dumas, *The Three Musketeers*. |
| 1829 | End of Russo-Turkish War. Creation of Metropolitan Police Force in London. Stephenson's *Rocket* wins the Rainhill locomotive trials. | Delacroix, *Sardanapaulus*. Rossini, *Guillaume Tell*. |

| Year | Age | Life |
|------|-----|------|
| 1830 | 24 | 10 June: IKB elected fellow of the Royal Society. |
| 1831 | 25 | 31 March: IKB appointed Engineer to the Clifton Bridge, Bristol.<br>June: Construction of Clifton Bridge begins.<br>October: IKB caught up in the Bristol Riots.<br>IKB builds observatory for Sir James South.<br>Wins commissions for new dock works at Monkwearmouth in Sunderland. |
| 1833 | 27 | 7 March: IKB appointed Engineer to the Great Western Railway, and undertakes preliminary survey of London-Bristol route. |
| 1835 | 29 | Work resumes on the Thames Tunnel (under direction of MIB). Work on Monkwearmouth docks begins, although much reduced in scope.<br>Great Western Steamship Company forms. |
| 1836 | 30 | 5 July: IKB marries Mary Horsley, and they move in to the floors above his Duke Street offices in Mayfair.<br>27 August: Foundation stone of Leigh abutment of Clifton Bridge laid.<br>Work starts on *Great Western*.<br>Work starts on the Box Tunnel. |

| Year | History | Culture |
|------|---------|---------|
| 1830 | Revolution in Paris.<br>Formal opening of Liverpool-<br>Manchester Railway. | Delacroix, *Liberty Guiding the People*.<br>Stendhal, *Le Rouge et Le Noir*. |
| 1831 | Belgium separates from the Netherlands.<br>Introduction of Reform Bill in Parliament. | Disraeli, *The Young Duke*. |
| 1833 | Death of locomotive inventor Richard Trevithick.<br>Slavery abolished in the British Empire. | Hugo, *The Hunchback of Notre Dame*. |
| 1835 | First railway line in Germany opens between Nuremberg and Furth.<br>1,098 miles of railway in use in USA. | Constable, *The Valley Farm*.<br>Donizetti, *Lucia di Lammermoor*. |
| 1836 | Chartist movement begins in Britain.<br>Battle of the Alamo in Texas.<br>John Ericsson patents screw propeller in the USA. | Marryat, *Mr Midshipman Easy*.<br>Dickens, *The Pickwick Papers*. |

| Year | Age | Life |
|------|-----|------|
| 1837 | 31 | 18 May: Isambard III, first son of IKB and Mary, is born. <br> 19 July: Launch of the *Great Western* in Bristol. |
| 1838 | 32 | 23 April: *Great Western* crosses the Atlantic in 15 days. <br> 4 June: First section of GWR opens, to Taplow. <br> IKB begins designs for the *Great Britain*. |
| 1841 | 35 | MIB knighted by Queen Victoria for his work on the Thames Tunnel. <br> 30 June: GWR completed between London and Bristol. <br> Work begins on the *Great Britain*. |
| 1842 | 36 | 1 July: First section of Bristol & Exeter Railway opened. <br> IKB recommends the use of the atmospheric system for the South Devon railway. |
| 1843 | 37 | 25 March: Thames Tunnel opened. <br> 19 July: Launch of the *SS Great Britain* in Bristol, on maiden voyage to New York . <br> The gauge war: conflict over the use of broad and narrow gauge in British railways intensifies. |
| 1846 | 40 | 22 September: *Great Britain* run aground in Dundrum Bay, Ireland. <br> Parliament passes the Gauge Act, effectively ruling out Brunel's broad-gauge system. |

| Year | History | Culture |
|------|---------|---------|
| 1837 | Accession to throne of Queen Victoria. First Canadian railway opens. | Carlyle, *The French Revolution*. |
| 1838 | First British-Afghan War. Formation of Anti-Corn Law League. | Dickens, *Oliver Twist* and *Nicholas Nickleby*. |
| 1841 | Sir Robert Peel becomes Prime Minister. First issue of Bradshaw's Railway Guide. | Dickens, *The Old Curiosity Shop*. Rossini, *Stabat Mater*. |
| 1842 | End of Opium War between Britain and China. Queen Victoria makes her first railway journey, from Windsor to Paddington. | Poe, *The Masque of the Red Death*. Glinka, *Ruslan and Ludmilla*. |
| 1843 | Maori revolt against British in New Zealand. | Dickens, *A Christmas Carol*. Tennyson, *Mort d'Arthur*. |
| 1846 | End of First Sikh War in India. Irish Potato Famine begins. | Edward Lear, *Book of Nonsense*. Berlioz, *Damnation of Faust*. |

| Year | Age | Life |
|------|-----|------|
| 1847 | 41 | 27 August: *Great Britain* refloated.<br>3 September First atmospheric train runs between Exeter and Teignmouth. |
| 1848 | 42 | Construction of Saltash Bridge begins. |
| 1849 | 43 | Atmospheric system abandoned.<br>12 December: MIB dies. |
| 1852 | 46 | 25 March: IKB makes his first sketches for the *Great Eastern*.<br>July: Chepstow Bridge opens.<br>Work begins on Paddington station.<br>*Great Britain* inaugurates first regular steamship service to Australia |
| 1853 | 47 | Work begins on SS *Great Eastern* (in partnership with John Scott Russell) and Royal Albert Bridge. |
| 1854 | 48 | 16 January: Paddington New Station opened. |
| 1855 | 49 | IKB designs prefabricated hospital at Renkioi for soldiers of the Crimean War. The SS *Great Britain* carries troops. |

| Year | History | Culture |
| --- | --- | --- |
| 1847 | Mexican War: US forces capture Mexico City. Factory Act in Britain limits working hours of women and children. | Thackeray, *Vanity Fair*. Charlotte Brontë, *Jane Eyre*. Verdi, *Macbeth*. |
| 1848 | The Year of Revolutions: uprisings in Paris, Vienna and Berlin. First Public Health Act in Britain. | Millais, *Ophelia*. Macaulay, *History of England*. |
| 1849 | British victory in Second Sikh War. | Dickens, *David Copperfield*. |
| 1852 | Louis-Napoleon declares himself Emperor Napoleon III. Death of the Duke of Wellington. | Stowe, *Uncle Tom's Cabin*. |
| 1853 | Outbreak of war between Russia and the Ottoman Empire. First railway through the Alps (Vienna–Trieste). | Verdi, *Il Trovatore and La Traviata*. |
| 1854 | The Crimean War: Britain and France ally with Ottoman Empire and declare war on Russia. | Kingsley, *Westward Ho*. Tennyson, *The Charge of the Light Brigade*. |
| 1855 | The Crimean War: Russians surrender at Sebastopol. | Dickens, *Little Dorrit*. Trollope, *The Warden*. |

| Year | Age | Life |
|------|-----|------|
| 1857 | 51 | *Great Western* broken up.<br>*Great Britain* carries troops to Indian Mutiny.<br>3 November: Attempts at launching the<br>*Great Eastern* begin. |
| 1858 | 52 | 31 January: SS *Great Eastern* is finally launched.<br>Another company is created to complete her<br>furnishings.<br>IKB shows signs of failing health and is advised by<br>his doctor to overwinter in Egypt. |
| 1859 | 53 | 11 April: Royal Albert Bridge, Saltash, completed<br>and opened while Brunel is still abroad in Egypt.<br>5 September: IKB goes to inspect the SS *Great<br>Eastern* two days before her launch. He collapses on<br>the deck and is taken home.<br>7 September: Launch of the *SS Great Eastern*.<br>Two days later, on 9 September, an explosion on<br>board during maiden voyage kills five and severely<br>injures 12.<br>15 September: IKB dies, at home at Duke Street. |
| 1864 | 54 | 8 Decembe: Clifton Bridge opened. |

| Year | History | Culture |
|------|---------|---------|
| 1857 | Indian Mutiny breaks out. Science Museum opens in London. | Hughes, *Tom Brown's Schooldays*. Baudelaire, *Les Fleurs du Mal*. |
| 1858 | End of Indian Mutiny. Suez Canal Company formed. | Carlyle, *Frederick the Great*. William P Firth, *Derby Day*. |
| 1859 | Franco-Austrian War. Work begins on the Suez Canal | Darwin, *On the Origin of Species by Natural Selection*. Dickens, *A Tale of Two Cities*. |
| 1864 | American Civil War: U S Grant become Union C-in-C. Schleswig-Holstein War. | Tolstoy, *War and Peace*. Dickens, *Our Mutual Friend*. |

# Further Reading

## Primary Sources

The Brunel Collection at the University of Bristol, Special Collections, is the richest source of information pertaining to Brunel. It was begun with a donation in the 1950s by Lady Celia Noble (Brunel's granddaughter) of Brunel's letterbooks, sketchbooks, documents and diaries and is still expanding. Most revealing about Brunel's character are the private and personal diaries. There is also a large collection of letters, including some from Brunel's youngest son, Henry, to his mother Mary, which provide an insight into the less-well known family life of the Brunels.

### Isambard's diaries (1824–1859)
Private Diaries, 1824–1826, 2 volumes
Thames Tunnel Journals, 1826–1829, 3 volumes
Personal Diary, 1827–1829, 1 volume
Private Diaries, 1830–1840, 2 volumes
Office Diaries (appointments only), 1833–1859, 25 volumes

### Sketchbooks (1830–1857)
Small Sketchbooks, c. 1837–1856, 17 volumes
Large Sketchbooks, 1830–1857, 17 volumes
Great Western Railway Sketchbooks, 1836–1842, 18 volumes
Other Sketchbooks, 1835–c.1836, 5 volumes

### Letters from Brunel (1830–1858)
To various correspondents including Charles Babbage (1791–1871),

Christopher Claxton (b.1790), Sir Daniel Gooch (1816–1889), Thomas Guppy (c.1797–1882), Sir Joseph Paxton (1801–1865), Henry Petty-Fitzmaurice, and Joseph D'Aguilar Samuda (1813–1885). There are also many letters from these correspondents to Brunel, concerning subjects aush as the Great Western Railway, Bristol Docks and Clifton Suspension Bridge.

**Letters to Brunel (1831–1859)**
From various correspondents including Michael Faraday (1791–1867), Dionysius Lardner (1793–1859), Sir Bradford Leslie (1831–1926), Charles Alexander Saunders (fl. 1830s–1850s) and Robert Stephenson (1819–1905). These cover such subjects as the Great Eastern and Great Britain steamships, and the Great Western Railway.

**Brunel family Correspondence (1836–1858)**
Including letters to and from Sir Benjamin Hawes (1797–1862), John Callcott Horsley (1817–1903) and his family, including Mary Horsley, Brunel's sister, as well as William Horsley (1774–1858).

## Secondary Sources

Beamish, Richard: *Memoir of the Life of Sir Marc Isambard Brunel* (1862) – Memoir of Marc Brunel's work in France, America and England, written by one of his assistant engineers on the Thames Tunnel.

Bryan, Tim: *Brunel, The Great Engineer* (Ian Allan Publishing, Surrey: 1999) – A brisk yet factually detailed book, with many fascinating pictures, by one of the leading experts on the Great Western Railway.

Bryan, Tim: *Railway Heritage: Paddington, Great Western Gateway* (Silver Link Publishing, Kettering: 1997).

Buchanan, Angus: *Brunel, The Life and Times of Isambard Kingdom Brunel* (Hambledon and London, London: 2002) – An insightful and thorough account of Brunel's life, wonderfully illuminated by extensive description of the historical context within which Brunel was working. This book present a balanced appraisal of Brunel's work, following some of the criticisms presented by Adrian Vaughan in his book *Isambard Kingdom Brunel, Engineering Knight Errant.*

Buck, Alan: *The Little Giant: A Life of I.K. Brunel* (David & Charles, Newton Abbot: 1986) – A dramatised version of Brunel's life, told as a novel.

Cadbury, Deborah: *Seven Wonders of the Industrial World,* (Harper Perennial, London: 2004) – Chapter One of this book tells the story of Brunel's largest ship, the *Great Eastern*, in very detailed and entertaining form.

Kentley, Eric (ed): *Isambard Kingdom Brunel, Recent Works* (Design Museum, London: 2000) – contains eight essays by eight experts on Brunel's primary works, each of which is followed by a 'project assessment' by a leading architect or engineer, appropriate to the construction. This book contains wonderful pictures and illustrations, and provides technical insight into Brunel's projects and an intriguing objective assessment to his achievements.

Mathewson, Richard and Laval, Derek: *Brunel's Tunnel . . . and where it led* (Brunel Exhibition Rotherhithe, 1992) – A short but detailed account of the building of the Thames Tunnel, with interesting comparisons to other tunnels from the era and from the present. *Available from the National Maritime Museum in Greenwich (London) and from the Brunel Engine House (museum of the Thames Tunnel), Rotherhithe (London).*

Noble, Celia: *The Brunels, Father & Son,* (Cobden Sanderson, London: 1838) – a more personal perspective on the Brunels, written by Isambard's granddaughter. Lady Noble had access to papers and documents that have since disappeared.

Pudney, John: *Brunel and his World* (Thames and Hudson, London: 1974) – a clear survey of Brunel's life with many illustrations.

Rolt, L T C: *Isambard Kingdom Brunel* (Penguin, London: 1989, 4th ed) – an exceptionally detailed and fond biography of Brunel. Rolt had exclusive access to papers that have not been available since he first wrote his book in 1957.

Simmons, Jack (ed): *The Birth of the Great Western Railway, Extracts from the Diary and Correspondence of George Henry Gibbs* (Adams & Dart, Bath: 1971) – the diaries of George Henry Gibbs, who sat on the London Board of Directors of the Great Western Railway, and was a loyal supporter of Brunel's, provide a fascinating alternative perspective of the events from 1836 to 1840, when the railway was being founded.

Simmons, Jack: *The Railways of Britain*, (2nd ed, London 1968) – a definitive book by the leading historian on the history of railways in Britain.

Vaughan, Adrian: *Isambard Kingdom Brunel, Engineering Knight Errant* (John Murray, London: 3rd ed, 2003) – an original account of Brunel's life which is fascinating because of the more critical approach it takes to Brunel and his working practices. Vaughan is sceptical of the rosy picture painted of Brunel, particularly by L T C Rolt (whose book *Brunel* was long regarded the definitive biography of Brunel) and suggests that while Brunel was undeniably a man of genius, his achievements were often gained at the expense of others' welfare and reputation.

Wilson, Roger Burdett (ed): *Sir Daniel Gooch: Memoirs and his Diary* (David & Charles, Newton Abbot, 1972) – the memoirs of the man who designed the greatest locomotives for Brunel's Great Western Railway.

# Picture Sources

The author and publishers wish to express their thanks to the following sources of illustrative material and/or permission to reproduce it. They will make the proper acknowledgements in future editions in the event that any omissions have occurred.

# Index